INTERNATIONAL DEVELOPMENT IN FOCUS

Moving Forward
Connectivity and Logistics to Sustain Bangladesh's Success

Matías Herrera Dappe, Charles Kunaka,
Mathilde Lebrand, and Nora Weisskopf

 **WORLD BANK GROUP**

Contents

Maps

Tables

Foreword

Logistics performance, especially supply chain efficiency, has become one of the ingredients for trade competitiveness and export growth and diversification. Improving logistics performance will help Bangladesh maintain its position as a major player in ready-made garments and, more importantly, help it diversify its export basket.

International experience shows the importance of a sound knowledge base in the design of logistics improvements strategies. This publication is the first comprehensive assessment of the logistics environment in Bangladesh. It explores the attributes of the major system components, including hard infrastructure and services, and analyzes how the system performs in terms of logistics costs. It estimates the demand for logistics based on an innovative modeling of freight flows that provides insights into the patterns of the flows of goods across space and their main drivers. The spatial picture of flows, combined with system attributes, helps improve the targeting of investments and measures.

The report provides some striking results. The picture that emerges is one of a system that is bursting at the seams, where demand for both infrastructure and services has long exceeded supply. One of the manifestations of this imbalance is congestion, especially on roads and highways. Congestion is most acute on the core corridor that links the economic heartland of the Dhaka region and the main trade gateway of Chittagong. Inadequate capacity is also evident in the poor reliability of services, which increases costs for private firms, which are forced to keep higher levels of inventory than do firms in other middle-income economies. The evidence also shows that Bangladesh is not exploiting the comparative advantages of rail and inland water transport, relying mainly on road transport, which contributes to the challenges faced by the system.

Several factors complicate the design of solutions to address the main weaknesses of the country's transport and logistics system. The number of government agencies involved in logistics is high in Bangladesh. In other countries, efforts of different groups of stakeholders are integrated and coordinated through a high-level logistics mechanism. Such a mechanism is lacking in Bangladesh. Bangladesh also suffers from many intermediaries, who distort markets, increase costs, and lower the quality of service.

The report offers pragmatic proposals to address the weaknesses in Bangladesh's logistics system and to make the sector more dynamic, so that it can continue to meet the needs of a growing economy. They include adopting a clear strategy, investing in core infrastructure in a more balanced manner across modes of transport, increasing system capacity, increasing competition in markets for logistics services, building the skills of logistics services providers, and tapping the potential of regional trade in South Asia, which is projected to grow. Improving logistics performance in Bangladesh would boost trade, supporting Bangladesh on its path to becoming a dynamic middle-income country, building on an increasingly dynamic private sector.

Readers, especially policy makers, will find this report a valuable resource for identifying what needs to be done to enhance logistics performance and conceive a more dynamic and efficient system that supports the country's record of robust growth and industrialization.

Mercy Tembon
Country Director for Bangladesh and Bhutan
The World Bank

Acknowledgments

This report was prepared by a team led by Matías Herrera Dappe (Senior Economist, Transport Global Practice). The core team included Charles Kunaka (Lead Specialist, Macro, Trade and Investment Global Practice); Mathilde Lebrand (Economist, Transport Global Practice); and Nora Weisskopf (former Transport Specialist, Transport Global Practice).

Joy Deep Chakrabartty, Aminul Islam, M. Shafiqul Islam, Moutushi Islam, Jonathan Kastelic, Akib Khan, Daniel Monchuk, Anisur Rahman, and Mehnaz Sanjana helped identify, collect, and assemble the data. Tateishi Eigo provided mapping support. Nasreen Begum, Md. Tafazzal Hossain, Habiba Jeba, Tema Alawari Kio-Michael, and Rex Quiah provided administrative support. Barbara Karni edited the report.

Prof. José Holguín-Veras, Juvena Ng Huiting, Lokesh Kumar Kalahasthi, Trilce Encarnación, Jeffrey Wojtowicz, Abdelrahman Ismael, Wilfredo F. Yushimito, Carlos I. Rivera-González, Carlos A. González-Calderón, and Xia Yang (all at Rensselaer Polytechnic Institute); Prof. Shamsul Hoque (Bangladesh University of Engineering and Technology); and Manish Sharma and his team at PwC prepared background analysis.

The work was carried out in collaboration with the Bangladesh Bureau of Statistics (BBS). The team would like to acknowledge the support of the BBS in providing access to the primary microdata sources used in the report, including the Economic Census and the Agriculture Census.

The team also appreciates helpful contributions, comments, and suggestions by the following colleagues: Farhad Ahmed, Muneeza Mehmood Alam, Bernard Aritua, Nusrat Nahid Babi, Ninan Oommen Biju, Brian Blankespoor, Hei Chiu, Simon Davies, Harrie de Leijer, Dilshad Dossani, Pablo Fajgelbaum (UCLA), Thomas Farole, Virgilio Galdo, Madhur Gautam, Richard Martin Humphreys, Zahid Hussain, Sanjay Kathuria, Yue Li, Muthukumara Mani, Sevara Melibaeva, Diep Nguyen-Van Houtte, Erik Nora, Jose Eduardo Gutierrez Ossio, Masrur Reaz, Mark Roberts, Rajesh Rohatgi, Julie Rozenberg, Shigeyuki Sakaki, Harris Selod, and Sanjay Srivastava.

The team is grateful to Robert Saum, Martin Rama, Shomik Mehndiratta, and Karla Gonzalez Carvajal for their support and guidance. Peer reviewers Megersa Abera Abate, Cecilia Briceño-Garmendia, Luis Blancas, and Somik Lall provided insightful and constructive comments on the draft report.

This work would not have been possible without financial support from the Partnership for South Asia Trust Fund, administered by the World Bank, with a financial contribution from Australia's Department of Foreign Affairs and Trade; the Multi-Donor Trust Fund for Sustainable Logistics (MDTF-SL), also administered by the World Bank, with a financial contribution from the government of the Netherlands; and the World Bank Strategic Research Program, a Multi-Donor Trust Fund, funded primarily by the United Kingdom's Department for International Development.

About the Authors

Matías Herrera Dappe is a Senior Economist in the Transport Global Practice of the World Bank, where he leads policy research programs on infrastructure. He has published extensively on infrastructure economics, transport connectivity, performance benchmarking, competition, and auctions. Before joining the World Bank, he worked for consulting firms and think tanks, advising governments and companies in Latin America, North America, and Europe. He holds a PhD in economics from the University of Maryland, College Park.

Charles Kunaka is a Lead Private Sector Specialist and Global Product Specialist on Connectivity and Logistics at the World Bank, where he leads several investment operations and projects on logistics and connectivity in the East Asia and Pacific, South Asia, and Africa regions. He has published extensively on connectivity and logistics topics, including trade and transport corridors, the Belt and Road Initiative, road transport services, and logistics. Between 2016 and 2019, he served as joint Secretary of the Global Infrastructure Connectivity Alliance, a G20 initiative to share knowledge and experience aimed at promoting an integrated and coherent connectivity agenda across the world. He holds an MSc in transport studies from Cranfield University and a PhD in transport studies from University College London.

Mathilde Lebrand is an Economist in the World Bank's Infrastructure Chief Economist Office, where she has been working on the Belt and Road Initiative, economic corridor development, and connectivity. Previously, she worked for the Europe and Central Asia Chief Economist Office where she contributed to several regional studies. Her research focuses on economic geography, transport, international trade, networks, and political economy. She has taught at the University of Montreal and worked at the World Trade Organization. She is a Research Fellow at the Center for Economic Studies ifo Institute (CESifo). She holds a PhD in economics from the European University Institute.

Nora Weisskopf is a Senior Program Manager at Amazon in the field of automation and supply chain optimization. Before joining Amazon, she was a Transport Specialist at the World Bank in Sydney, Australia, where her work covered a range of development-related transport and logistics issues, including the financing of transport and logistics infrastructure, operations, and policy as well as research in areas such as affordable and sustainable transport. She holds an MA in international business from the University of Edinburgh and a Master of Engineering in logistics from the Massachusetts Institute of Technology (MIT).

Abbreviations

BADC	Bangladesh Agricultural Development Corporation
BBA	Bangladesh Bridge Authority
BCIC	Bangladesh Chemical Industries Corporation
BICA	Bangladesh Inland Container Depot Association
BIWTA	Bangladesh Inland Water Transport Authority
BRTA	Bangladesh Road Transport Authority
BRTC	Bangladesh Road Transport Corporation
BSIC	Bangladesh Standard Industrial Classification
CHA	customs house agent
CO_2	carbon dioxide
DALY	disability-adjusted life year
DTCA	Dhaka Transport Coordination Authority
FODS	freight origin-destination synthesis
FTE	full-time equivalent
IMTP	Integrated Multimodal Transport Policy
IT	information technology
LGED	Local Government Engineering Department
MTE	medium truck equivalent
MVA	Motor Vehicles Agreement
NLTP	National Land Transport Policy
PIWTT	Protocol on Inland Water Transit and Trade
PPP	public-private partnership
RAJUK	Rajdhani Unnayan Kartripakkha
RHD	Road and Highways Department
TCI	Travel Congestion Index
TEU	20-foot equivalent unit
TFP	total factor productivity
VAT	value added tax

All tons are metric tons.

Overview

Bangladesh has been successful on many counts. The economy grew 6 percent a year between 2000 and 2017, and the poverty rate fell by more than half. All sectors experienced growth, but the contribution of agriculture to GDP declined, as Bangladesh became an important player in the textile and ready-made garments global value chain, which accounts for more than half of manufacturing employment and 84 percent of all exports in the country. Employment in the textile and ready-made garment sector grew 11 percent a year between 2003 and 2010, outpacing all other nonagricultural sectors (Farole and Cho 2017).

The sustainability of this growth model is now being challenged, as Bangladesh's competitiveness based on low wages is eroding. Rising wage demands from workers, intensifying global price competition, and inefficient logistics are putting significant cost pressure on Bangladeshi producers (Farole and Cho 2017). Since 2010 average annual employment growth in textile and ready-made garment sector has dropped to only 1.5 percent, and the rest of the economy has not been able to pick up the slack. Vietnam is doing a better job than Bangladesh of taking advantage of China's shift away from garments (World Bank 2018).

Bangladesh needs to increase its competitiveness to safeguard its comparative advantage in ready-made garments and diversify its exports basket. It ranked 99th among 137 countries on the World Economic Forum's Global Competitiveness Index for 2018, well behind other Asian countries, performing particularly poorly on transport and logistics. Bangladesh also underperforms other coastal countries in Asia on the World Bank's Logistics Performance Index. Improving logistics performance is thus an important lever with which to increase Bangladesh's competitiveness. Doing so would also help move the rural economy into high-value agricultural production, an important transition in a country in which agriculture will continue to play an important role in the economy.

This report presents a comprehensive assessment of logistics performance, its root causes, and the economic implications of potential interventions. Based on the analysis, it proposes policy directions to improve logistics performance.

Bangladesh does not systematically collect information on transport and logistics—a major constraint to improving the sector. To inform decision making, this report draws on many primary and secondary data sources—including censuses, specialized surveys of shippers and logistics service providers, and GPS tracking of road vehicles across the country—which it analyzes with state-of-the-art modeling techniques.

CONGESTED, UNRELIABLE, AND UNSOPHISTICATED: BANGLADESH'S LOGISTICS SYSTEM IMPOSES HIGH COSTS ON THE ECONOMY

Logistics costs in Bangladesh are high in most sectors, ranging from 4.5 percent of sales (for leather footwear) to 47.9 percent of sales (for horticulture). Inventory carrying costs represent a significant share of logistics costs (figure O.1). Transport represents the largest share of direct logistics costs, and road transport is the dominant transport mode. Road transport rates in Bangladesh range from $0.06 for a 16-ton truck to $0.12 for a trailer. They are higher than in many developing and developed countries.

Congested and unreliable logistics system

Congestion and delays are pervasive problems across the national logistics system, from roads to seaports and land ports. Congestion on roads alone doubles standard trucking costs.[1] Data from GPS devices that were fitted on trucks indicate that the average speed is about 19 kilometers an hour—less than half what it would have been under uncongested conditions. If there were no congestion on roads, logistics costs would be at least 7–35 percent lower, depending on the sector. Average dwell times at Chattogram Port are 4 days for an export container and 11 days for an import container. Reducing dwell times would reduce logistics costs significantly.

FIGURE O.1

Logistics costs in Bangladesh, by industry

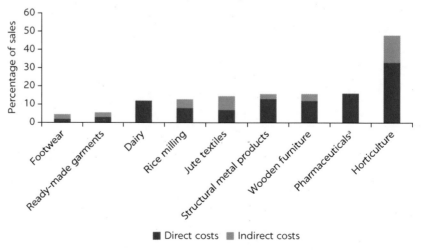

Source: World Bank analysis.
a. Logistics costs for the pharmaceutical industry include only direct costs, as firms did not provide the information required to estimate inventory carrying costs.

The dominant role of road transport and congestion impose additional costs on society. The social costs of annual carbon dioxide (CO_2) emissions from inter-district road freight transport in Bangladesh is equivalent to 1.2 percent of GDP, with almost 60 percent of the emissions caused by congestion.

Shippers and service providers take costly actions to cope with congestion and unreliability in the logistics system. Industries hold large inventories of raw materials and finished goods. Inventory carrying costs represent 17–56 percent of logistics costs; in most industries the figure exceeds 30 percent. The shares of inventory affected by inconsistent deliveries and congestion are very high, ranging from 53 to 75 percent, depending on the industry. Export-oriented industries and industries relying on imported inputs—such as ready-made garments, footwear, and pharmaceuticals—need to maintain higher levels of inventories (up to six months) to mitigate the impact of unreliable deliveries and higher lead time caused by congestion at Chattogram Port. To cope with unreliability and delays at ferry crossings, for example, truck operators make "facilitation payments" amounting to 11 percent of their operating costs, which they then pass on to shippers.

Congestion and unreliability are problems in Bangladesh because all elements of the core transport and logistics infrastructure lack adequate capacity for the traffic volumes they handle and are inefficiently operated, further reducing their effective capacity. In addition, Bangladesh's infrastructure is in poor condition. Maintaining infrastructure in good condition is difficult partly because of the high incidence of vehicle overloading and the country's exposure to natural disasters. Underinvestment in increasing capacity and maintenance of infrastructure is a contributory factor to the low speeds on roads and the poor reliability across modes.

Unsophisticated logistics system

Bangladesh's logistics system is unsophisticated. Efficient modern logistics systems are characterized by the use of different permutations of modes of transport in multimodal operations. Bangladesh's system is fragmented in terms of both logistics infrastructure and services. The core infrastructure for all modes of transport is in place, but there is a lack of intermodal facilities, and the few facilities that do exist are poorly operated.

Most logistics service providers are active in only one service category of logistics; use of multimodal transport is extremely limited. About 91 percent of shippers surveyed reported few to almost no instances in which logistics service providers use multimodal transport to reduce logistics cost. Shippers typically work with more than one service provider to complete each shipment.

Fragmented service providers are characterized by low skills, the poor quality of assets, and limited use of information technology (IT) tools, which are increasingly prevalent in many other countries. Eighty percent of shippers surveyed reported instances of unprofessional behavior by logistics service providers. Most truck drivers are low skilled and illiterate. In addition to reducing service quality, poor driving skills contribute to road crashes, which represent about 11 percent of truck operating costs. About 60 percent of shippers surveyed reported that service providers do not have the capability to track and trace shipments. Because of the low quality of services, many manufacturing firms provide their logistics needs in house to better control the performance of their supply chains.

FRAGMENTED, INEFFECTIVE, AND OUTDATED GOVERNANCE HAS LED TO INEFFICIENCIES IN LOGISTICS

The role of the government in the logistics sector is to create an environment that is conducive to efficient logistics. Through policies, planning, and regulations the government sets the direction and the rules of engagement for the public and private players in the logistics sector. Adequate and effective policies, planning, and regulations and their enforcement should solve coordination problems and tackle market failures, ensuring that public and private players face incentives to provide efficient infrastructure and services.

Fragmented governance

Nine ministries and more than 20 government agencies play roles in setting policies and regulations, planning, operating infrastructure, and providing services. The fragmented governance of the logistics sector exacerbates the coordination problem intrinsic to infrastructure development, leading to transport modes that developed and evolved in silos and basic mismatches of infrastructure standards, such as bridges that are narrower than approach roads. In the few cases where transport modes are connected, public operators work in silos, requiring shippers and service providers to submit the same information several times. Overlapping mandates and shared ownership have made the planning, construction, and maintenance of transport infrastructure more complex than it should be.

The lack of coordination leads to government-created externalities. Sectoral policies are set without considering their negative effects on the entire logistics system. A case in point is custom policies that lead to limited inland containerization. Customs allows only 37 commodities to be cleared outside the port, does not allow companies to open container freight stations at locations far from Chattogram Port, and treats empty containers as bonded goods. These policies lead to an increase in the number of vehicles on the roads, as 1.25 covered vans are required to transport the cargo in one 20-foot equivalent (TEU) container. The policies also increase congestion inside Chattogram Port, leading to inefficient port operation.

The fragmented governance and lack of coordination reflects the absence of an integrated logistics strategy and planning focused on efficiency. Each ministry and government agency make decisions and take actions to achieve its narrowly defined objectives. As a result, the higher-level objective of creating an efficient logistics sector is not achieved.

Ineffective governance

Bangladesh has been ineffective in tackling market failures in the logistics sector and in implementing and managing infrastructure.

Market failures

Logistics service markets in Bangladesh are not competitive. Thousands of operators, many of them using very small fleets or single units, provide trucking and inland water shipping operations. Drivers unions, owners associations, or brokers related to them set prices and control access to cargo, interfering with the market mechanism and preventing full competition. More than 85 percent of shippers interviewed believe there is no competition in logistics service markets

FIGURE O.2

Shippers' perceptions of competition in logistics service markets in Bangladesh

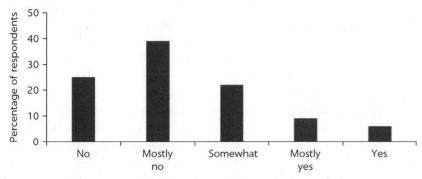

Source: Survey conducted for this report.

in Bangladesh (figure O.2). The involvement of unions and associations prevents direct interaction between service providers and shippers. As service providers are not rewarded for the quality of their services, they have no incentive to provide high-quality services or innovate.

The Competition Act aims to prevent collusion in the market and price fixing by industry players through various mechanisms, such as bid rigging, control over the supply of goods or services, and abuse of dominant position. However, the act has not yet been fully implemented, and the Bangladesh Competition Commission stipulated in the act is not yet functional.

Accidents caused by trucks and damage to road and bridge infrastructure from truck overloading are two important externalities. Regulations regarding the licensing of drivers and vehicles are meant to reduce accidents, but weak enforcement defeats the purpose of the regulations. Unqualified drivers driving heavy vehicles pay facilitation payments to obtain licenses. Modified or unfit trucks are issued fitness certificates. Transport operators often overload their trucks by more than 50 percent. When they are caught, carriers simply pay facilitation payments to traffic police and other monitoring authorities to avoid penalties. These practices have resulted in unskilled drivers, substandard trucks on the road, and overloading.

Logistics service providers also face hurdles in the business environment, limiting their ability to grow and deliver modern and sophisticated services. Service providers lack access to financing, because the financial sector in Bangladesh considers the sector risky and provides limited or only costly options for financing fleets and other assets. The informality in the sector and the lack of a tamper-proof centralized property registry for movable assets give rise to information asymmetries that curtail access to bank financing by logistics service providers, which the government could help solving.

Infrastructure implementation and management

Bangladesh has been inefficient in implementing and managing its infrastructure. Weak governance, including poor planning and implementation, and corruption are key factors behind the high cost of construction. Sectoral plans and policies focusing on the maintenance of transport infrastructure exist, but implementation has been slow. Without regular maintenance, infrastructure rapidly falls into disrepair, requiring expensive reconstruction to bring it back to adequate standards.

Outdated policies and regulations

The logistics sector suffers from outdated policies and regulations. Much of the legislation and regulations that govern transport and logistics services date back to the pre-independence period, when the economy was mainly agricultural.

One of the most important weaknesses of the policies in place is that they do not focus on services. The main sectoral policies focus mainly on the development of infrastructure for various subsectors. The modern national-level policies developed by many other countries address improvement of infrastructure, integration of various modes of transport, and improvement in the quality of services.

The infrastructure provision paradigm in place in Bangladesh gives the private sector a minor role in the financing, management, and operation of infrastructure. Bangladesh is the only country in South Asia where the landlord port model has not been implemented, for example. The Bangladesh Investment Development Authority, the principal private investment promotion and facilitation agency in Bangladesh, has not included infrastructure in the list of permitted foreign investments.

Restrictive policies toward foreign private participation in the provision of logistics services also hurt the sector. In many countries, international players take the lead in introducing innovative integrated logistics services. Multinational players that are willing to enter the logistics market in Bangladesh have to create joint ventures with local companies.

MAKING LOGISTICS MORE EFFICIENT WOULD SIGNIFICANTLY BOOST EXPORT GROWTH, WITH THE BENEFITS GOING LARGELY TO GREATER DHAKA

A comprehensive approach that reduces dwell times at Chattogram Port by one day; increases the minimum speed along national highways to 40 kilometers an hour; and implements logistics policies to tackle the low quality of logistics services, facilitation payments, and other inefficiencies could reduce logistics costs for tradables by 26 percent. Such a comprehensive approach would increase Bangladesh's exports by 19 percent.

Bangladesh's economic success has been unevenly distributed. Economic activity is concentrated in Greater Dhaka and Chattogram; other urban areas struggle to attract investments and workers. As a result, the northwest-southeast corridor is the backbone of the country. Freight flows on the Dhaka–Chattogram section, where international freight shipments dominate, are the heaviest in the country, followed by the Dhaka–northwest section, where domestic shipments dominate.

An important policy question is how the gains from improved logistics efficiency and increased competitiveness would be distributed across the country. Using a spatial general equilibrium model for Bangladesh, this study assesses the impact of improving internal connectivity and logistics on the integration of districts with global markets and their economic prospects. Different interventions in the comprehensive approach distribute the gains across districts differently, but all of them leverage the comparative advantage and livability of Greater Dhaka, increasing its prominence in the country. These results suggest that other forces—such as labor market density, agglomeration gains, and access to education, health, and other services—are important and that complementary policies in these areas might help increase the attractiveness of secondary cities.

Achieving efficient logistics requires a system-wide approach

The comprehensive diagnostic presented in this report yields one main conclusion: A system-wide approach is needed to increase logistics efficiency. The report provides high-level direction on the policy domains that may be considered when designing such an approach. The overarching objective of increasing logistics efficiency can be split into four interlinked objectives.

1. Developing a system-wide strategy for increasing logistics efficiency

Bangladesh needs a coherent, integrated logistics strategy and master plan that leverage the strengths of each of the elements of the system. The strategy should ensure coordination among all public institutions involved in logistics and be co-developed with private sector shippers and service providers. The integrated strategy and master plan should be based on robust data and accompanied by a robust data management system for monitoring and continuous improvement.

2. Improving the quality, capacity, and management of infrastructure

Connectivity needs to be improved by expanding existing links and building new ones. The solution is not just to invest more, however, but to invest better, by focusing on the service gap instead of the infrastructure gap and moving away from the build, neglect, rebuild mindset. Investing better also means increasing the resilience of the transport network to climate events. Improving the quality and management of infrastructure requires strengthening the regulatory framework and its enforcement. There is a need and an opportunity to rethink and improve the paradigm governing the provision of infrastructure services by allowing the private sector to play a larger role in the financing, management, and operation of infrastructure. The public sector will continue to play an important role in infrastructure provision and management. There is therefore a need to improve its management and implementation capacity, in order to get more out of scarce resources.

3. Improving the quality and integration of logistics services

Services can be upgraded by ensuring competition in markets. If service providers are remunerated based on the quality of their services, they will be incentivized to increase quality and innovate. Improving the quality and integration of logistics services also requires modernizing the regulatory framework and the procedures for trade and transport, insisting on minimum standards (without directly affecting the quantity of supply), and strengthening the enforcement of regulations. Helping breach information asymmetries between service providers and shippers, and between service providers and banks would also support the improvement and modernization of logistics services.

4. Achieving seamless regional connectivity

Bangladesh can leverage its strategic location in South Asia to serve as a regional logistics node. To do so, it needs to improve infrastructure and services; standardize and harmonize regulatory practices with neighbors; and reform policies and regulations to cover the cross-border movement of goods, vehicles, and drivers and ensure appropriate cost recovery for services and infrastructure. Integration agreements should follow best practices and use international legal instruments for harmonization.

NOTE

1. Standard trucking costs include the labor costs of the driver and helper; depreciation and interest; and the costs of fuel, insurance, registration, maintenance, and tires.

REFERENCES

Farole, T., and Y. Cho. 2017. *Jobs Diagnostic Bangladesh*. World Bank, Washington, DC.

World Bank. 2018. *Bangladesh Development Update: Building on Resilience*. Washington, DC.

——. 2019. *Doing Business*. Washington, DC.

1 Successful Albeit Poor Logistics Performance

INTRODUCTION

Bangladesh experienced sustained growth and poverty reduction over the last few decades. GDP grew at an average annual rate of 5.6 percent between 2000 and 2010 and 6.7 percent between 2010 and 2018. The national poverty rate fell by more than half between 2000 and 2016, to 24.3 percent (World Bank 2018a).

Gains in labor productivity and favorable demographics drove growth. Between 2003 and 2016, value added per worker grew 4.25 percent a year, accounting for three-quarters of overall growth in per capita value added; demographic change accounted for almost all of the remaining growth (Farole and Cho 2017). Although all sectors experienced growth, there was a shift in the contribution of agriculture and industry to GDP. The shift of workers from agriculture to industry and service accounted for more than a quarter of overall growth in value added per worker between 2003 and 2016. The main driver of labor productivity growth, however, came from within-sector changes, most notably in the services sector, which accounted for more than 40 percent of total growth (Farole and Cho 2017).

Labor productivity in all sectors remains extremely low by international standards, and the performance of the manufacturing sector is weak. Labor productivity in Bangladesh is half that of the South Asian average, less than 40 percent of the average lower-middle-income country, and less than 10 percent of the global average (Farole and Cho 2017). In the industrial sector, labor productivity grew at only half the level for the economy as a whole. Labor productivity in manufacturing was particularly weak, with average annual growth of just 1.6 percent in 2003–10 and 2.2 percent in 2010–16 (Farole and Cho 2017).

The pace of job creation and poverty reduction slowed sharply in recent years. Wage labor growth was a substantial driver of poverty reduction. However, between 2010 and 2016, employment grew more slowly than the working-age population, despite accelerating growth in real GDP per capita (Farole and Cho 2017). Employment in the ready-made garment and textile sectors grew at 11 percent a year in 2003–10, outpacing all other nonagricultural sectors. After 2010 the growth rate of employment in the sectors dropped to only 1.5 percent a year. Employment in other manufacturing sectors has been growing rapidly (figure 1.1). However, given the massive scale of the

FIGURE 1.1

Average annual growth in employment of nonagricultural sectors in Bangladesh, 2003–10 and 2010–16

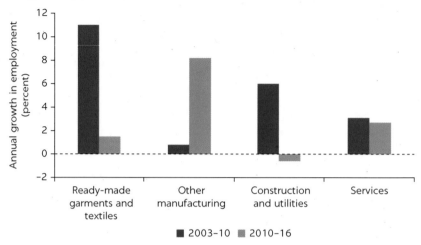

Source: Farole and Cho 2017.

ready-made garment and textiles sectors—which together account for 54 percent of all manufacturing jobs—employment growth in other manufacturing sectors is not sufficient to offset the slowdown in those sectors. The amount of poverty reduction achieved by each percent of growth fell by a third after 2010 (World Bank 2018a).

UNEVENLY DISTRIBUTED SUCCESS

Traditionally, western Bangladesh has lagged behind the eastern part of the country. Before the construction of the Bangabandhu Bridge, in 1998, travelling between east and west required crossing the Jamuna or Padma rivers by ferry. Limited connectivity meant the western districts were far away from the capital city of Dhaka and the main sea port (Chattogram), as the travel time and cost to reach them were high.

In 1995/96 the share of the population whose income was below the poverty line was 61 percent in the northwest region and 40 percent around Dhaka (Blankespoor and others 2018). Construction of the Bangabandhu Bridge brought significant benefits to the west, particularly the northwest (Blankespoor and others 2018), narrowing this difference. Disparities remain, however. Poverty in the southwest is still higher than in most eastern districts (map 1.1), and stronger poverty reduction in the eastern region between 2010 and 2016 increased the east-west gap.

Economic activity is concentrated in Dhaka and Chattogram. About 52 percent of employment in industry and 16 percent of employment in services is based in the Greater Dhaka and Chattogram metropolitan area, where less than 15 percent of the population lives.[1] Almost 100 percent of exports of ready-made garments are concentrated in Greater Dhaka and Chattogram. Most other districts produce agricultural goods and services for local markets. Nighttime light intensity per capita across the country highlights the concentration of economic activity around the capital (map 1.2).

MAP 1.1

Poverty rates in Bangladesh, by district

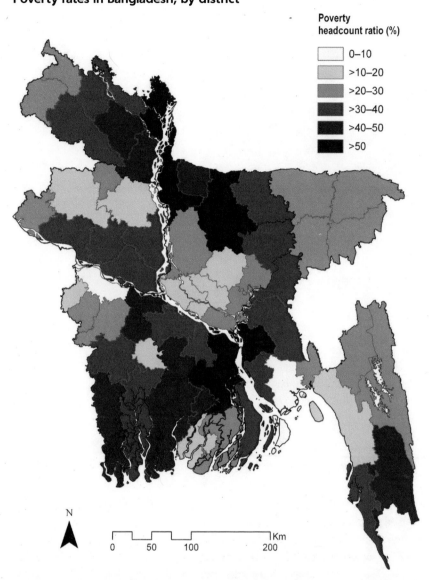

**Poverty
headcount ratio (%)**

	0–10
	>10–20
	>20–30
	>30–40
	>40–50
	>50

Source: World Bank Bangladesh Interactive Poverty Maps database.
Note: This map was constructed by combining the 2010 Bangladesh Poverty Maps, the IPUMS sample from the 2011 Bangladesh Census of Population and Housing, and the 2012 Undernutrition Maps of Bangladesh.

Bangladesh lacks thriving secondary cities. The presence of scale economies in industrial production and easier access to workers and service providers explain the agglomeration of activities in a few locations. As Dhaka becomes increasingly congested, the expectation is that manufacturing shifts to the periphery and that secondary cities begin to become more attractive locations for manufacturing. The latter does not appear to be happening in Bangladesh, raising questions about the environment for investment and job creation in Bangladesh's secondary cities. Outside Dhaka most nonagricultural employment growth is in relatively low-productivity services jobs. Although there is less congestion in secondary cities than in Dhaka and Chattogram, secondary cities face even greater shortfalls in critical infrastructure.

MAP 1.2

Nighttime light intensity per capita in Bangladesh, by district

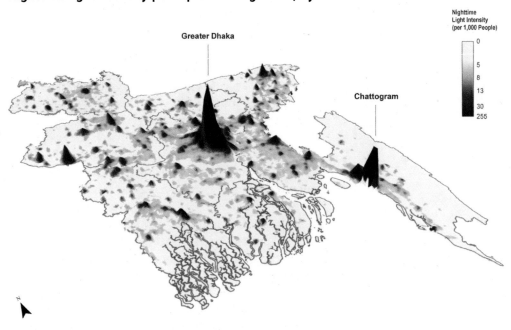

Nighttime
Light Intensity
(per 1,000 People)

0
5
8
13
30
255

Source: Bird and others 2018.

Garment firms perceive secondary cities as uncompetitive distant places, with poor access to markets and skilled labor as their main disadvantage (Muzzini and Aparicio 2013).

THE NEED TO IMPROVE LOGISTICS PERFORMANCE

There is still significant potential for the ready-made garment sector to keep growing and creating more jobs. Changes in global demand and supply could benefit South Asia, particularly Bangladesh. Given rising wages in China, Chinese investors are seeking to source from Bangladesh. Both China and India are diversifying away from garments, giving Bangladesh an opportunity not only to increase its world market share in garments but also to find markets in these countries. Lopez-Acevedo and Robertson (2016) estimate that a 10 percent increase in Chinese apparel prices would result in a 13.6 percent rise in Bangladesh's apparel exports to the United States and increase employment in the apparel sector in Bangladesh by 4.2 percent.

Employment trends underscore the importance of diversification in manufacturing, particularly exports. The ready-made garment and textile sectors account for 84 percent of all goods exports from Bangladesh. Other products, including jute goods, footwear, seafood, leather products, and pharmaceuticals, are emerging (Kathuria and Malouche 2015), but Bangladesh has not diversified its export basket as much as peer countries, such as Vietnam, have. There is evidence to suggest that Bangladesh's industrial and trade policy environment favored ready-made garments over other sectors (Davies and Butterworth 2015; Kathuria and Malouche 2016). Other factors that contributed to the failure to diversify exports include business regulatory constraints, lack of access to land, skills gaps, and poor logistics.

Bangladesh remains less competitive than other Asian countries, and its competitiveness based on low wages is eroding. Bangladesh ranked 99th among 137 countries in the World Economic Forum's (WEF) Global Competitiveness Index for 2018, well behind all but Pakistan in South Asia and all of its competitors in East Asia. Rising wage demands from workers, intensifying global price competition, and inefficient logistics are putting significant cost pressure on Bangladeshi producers (Farole and Cho 2017). Vietnam is doing a much better job of taking advantage of China's displacement (World Bank 2018a).

Improving logistics is key to improving Bangladesh's competitiveness. Efficient logistics reduce costs and delays for exports and expedite imports of consumer goods and foreign inputs used in domestic production. Superior logistics performance offers countries a competitive advantage in an era of growing globalization, increases production sharing across countries, and shortens product lifecycles.

Despite some progress in improving its logistics performance, Bangladesh still lags its main competitors (figure 1.2). It trails India and Vietnam in every aspect, especially infrastructure and customs. Many garment firms report inefficient logistics as one of the main constraints to servicing the orders they receive (Lopez-Acevedo and Robertson 2016).

Efficient logistics supports diversification into high-value agriculture. Despite the structural transformation, agriculture will continue playing an important role in the economy. But diversification into high-value agriculture (horticulture, livestock, and fisheries products) has been slow in Bangladesh (Gautam and Faruqee 2016). Farmers remain heavily invested in rice, even though nonrice crops and noncrop agriculture offer significantly higher incomes. Physical infrastructure and value chain inefficiencies are some of the constraints slowing diversification.

Better connectivity and logistics performance would help achieve a better allocation of production inputs across sectors, firms, and districts. Misallocation of resources across firms is one of the main sources of differences in total factor productivity (TFP) across countries. Hsieh and Klenow (2009) show that differences between the marginal products of factors caused by misallocation may account for up to 60 percent of the TFP gap between India and the United States. TFP growth in Bangladesh averaged just 0.7 percent between 2003 and

FIGURE 1.2

Logistics Performance Index (LPI) for selected countries, 2018

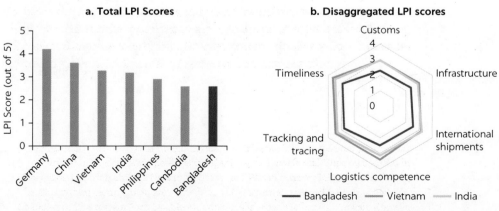

Source: World Bank 2018b.

2015—only one-sixth of labor productivity growth—indicating that much of labor productivity growth was driven by capital accumulation rather than efficiency in resource allocation (Sinha 2017). The highway investment along the Golden Quadrilateral in India led to real income gains of 2.7 percent, with a better allocation of factors accounting for 7.4 percent of those gains (Asturias, García-Santana, and Ramos Magdaleno 2018). High transport costs and poor logistics prevent firms from choosing optimal locations and keep production factors from being optimally allocated across sectors and regions.

LOGISTICS DIAGNOSTIC

Understanding the performance of the logistics sector and its drivers and designing the optimal policies and investments to improve it require a comprehensive diagnostic that looks at the supply of and demand for infrastructure and services. A logistics diagnostic should put the user at the center and go beyond direct costs to include indirect or opportunity costs. A national-level logistics diagnostic should also look at the externalities of logistics, such as pollution, and their costs to society.

This report presents a comprehensive diagnostic of the logistics sector in Bangladesh and recommends options for tackling the inefficiencies identified. The analysis looks at the factors that determine the stock and quality of infrastructure and the factors that determine the demand for different kinds of infrastructure in different parts of the country. It examines the incentives to provide logistics services of a certain type and quality and to charge the observed prices, which are affected by the infrastructure in place, the procedures for trade and transport, the market structure, and regulations, among other factors (figure 1.3). The analysis also looks at the drivers of demand for logistics services. The report quantifies the potential impacts of removing transport and logistics

FIGURE 1.3

Framework for analyzing logistics costs

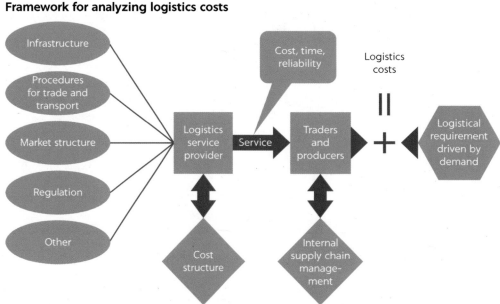

Source: Arvis, Raballand, and Marteau 2010.

TABLE 1.1 **Summary of main data used in the logistics diagnostic**

TYPE AND SOURCE OF DATA	YEARS COVERED
Secondary data	
Agriculture Census (Bangladesh Bureau of Statistics)	2008
Economic Census (Bangladesh Bureau of Statistics)	2013
Rail freight movements (Bangladesh Railways)	2016–17
Road traffic (Road and Highways Department)	2013
Primary data	
Freight Generation Survey	2017
Truck movements	2017–18
Logistics Users Survey	2017
Logistics Service Providers Survey	2017

Source: World Bank.

inefficiencies through various means on exports and the economic geography of Bangladesh.

The logistics diagnostic uses a novel and wide-ranging dataset. A logistics diagnostic needs to be based on detailed micro data instead of the usual aggregate metrics. It should combine quantitative and qualitative data to identify where inefficiencies are and how they affect the economy.

One weakness in Bangladesh has been the lack of reliable and current data to guide policy and project design in the transport and logistics sector (ADB 2012). To address the problem, this report collected both primary and secondary data (table 1.1).

ORGANIZATION OF THE REPORT

The report is organized as follows. Chapter 1 provides the economic context and motivation for the logistics diagnostic. Chapter 2 presents a comprehensive analysis of freight demand based on a novel freight model for Bangladesh. Chapter 3 quantifies logistics costs and the costs of logistics externalities and identifies their main drivers. Chapter 4 identifies and discusses the main inefficiencies in freight transport and logistics infrastructure. Chapter 5 identifies and discusses the main inefficiencies in freight transport and logistics services. Chapter 6 estimates the spatial economic effects of interventions to reduce logistics costs and improve connectivity. Chapter 7 presents policy options for removing inefficiencies in transport and logistics infrastructure and services.

NOTE

1. Greater Dhaka is defined by the Dhaka City Corporation; the Savar and Keraniganj *upazilas* (subdistricts) in Dhaka district; the Narayanganj, Sadar, Bandar, and Rupganj upazilas in Narayanganj district; and the Narsingdi, Sadar, and Palash *upazilas* in Narsingdi district. The Chattogram metropolitan area is defined as the *upazilas* of Bayejid, Bostami, Bakalia, Chandgaon, Chattogram Port, Double Mooring, Halishahar, Hathazari, Kotwali, Khulshi, Pahartali, Panchlaish, Patiya, Patenga, and Sitakunda in Chattogram district.

REFERENCES

ADB (Asian Development Bank). 2012. *Capacity Building and Support to the Transport Sector Coordination Wing of the Planning Commission.* Manila.

Arvis, J. F., G. Raballand, and J. F. Marteau. 2010. *The Cost of Being Landlocked: Logistics Costs and Supply Chain Reliability. Directions in Development.* Washington, DC: World Bank.

Asturias, J. M. García-Santana, and R. R. Magdaleno. 2018. "Competition and the Welfare Gains from Transportation Infrastructure: Evidence from the Golden Quadrilateral of India." Working Paper 1816, Banco de España, Madrid.

BBS (Bangladesh Bureau of Statistics). 2011. *Population and Housing Census 2011.* Statistics and Informatics Division, Ministry of Planning, Dhaka.

Bird, J., Y. Li, H. Z. Rahman, M. Rama, and A. J. Venables. 2018. *Toward Great Dhaka: A New Urban Development Paradigm Eastward.* Directions in Development. Washington, DC: World Bank.

Blankespoor, B., M. S. Emran, F. Shilpi, and L. Xu. 2018. "Bridge to Bigpush or Backwash? Market Integration, Reallocation, and Productivity Effects of Jamuna Bridge in Bangladesh." Policy Research Working Paper 8508, World Bank, Washington, DC.

Davies, S., and D. Butterworth. 2015. *Inclusive Growth Diagnostics.* Draft report. London: Department for International Development.

Farole, T., and Y. Cho. 2017. *Jobs Diagnostic Bangladesh.* World Bank, Washington, DC.

Gautam, M., and R. Faruqee. 2016. *Dynamics of Rural Growth in Bangladesh: Sustaining Poverty Reduction.* Directions in Development. Washington, DC: World Bank.

Hsieh, C., and P. J. Klenow. 2009. "Misallocation and Manufacturing TFP in China and India." *Quarterly Journal of Economics* 124 (4): 1403–48.

Kathuria, S., and M. M. Malouche. 2016. *Toward New Sources of Competitiveness in Bangladesh: Key Findings of the Diagnostic Trade Integration Study.* Directions in Development. Washington, DC: World Bank.

Li, Y., M. Rama, V. Galdo, and M. F. Pinto. 2015. "A Spatial Database for South Asia." Working Paper, World Bank, Washington, DC.

Lopez-Acevedo, G., and R. Robertson, eds. 2016. *Stitches to Riches? Apparel Employment, Trade, and Economic Development in South Asia.* Directions in Development. Washington, DC: World Bank.

Muzzini, E., and G. Aparicio. 2013. *Bangladesh: The Path to Middle-Income Status from an Urban Perspective.* Directions in Development. Washington, DC: World Bank.

NOAA (National Oceanic and Atmospheric Administration). 2010. "DSMP-OLS Radiance Calibrated Nighttime Lights." http://ngdc.noaa.gov/eog/dmsp/download_radcal.html.

Sinha, R. 2017. "Long-Term Growth Scenarios for Bangladesh." Policy Research Working Paper 7952, World Bank, Washington, DC.

World Bank. 2018a. *Bangladesh Development Update: Building on Resilience.* Washington, DC.

——. 2018b. *Logistics Performance Index.* Washington, DC.

2 Freight Demand

INTRODUCTION

Developing adequate infrastructure to serve users requires understanding demand and the forces driving it. For freight transport, it means understanding where freight is generated, how much is generated, where it is going, and how it is transported from origin to destination. Lack of planning or planning that is not based on proper demand analysis yields under- or over-supply of infrastructure (overly congested roads or roads in areas where there is no traffic).

Bangladesh benefits from a geography that allowed it to develop a multimodal transport network consisting of roads, railways, and waterways. However, its development was not based on a comprehensive assessment of demand, partly because of the lack of primary transport data sources for preparing and updating master plans (ADB 2012). There is no current origin-destination analysis of freight for the entire country—and hence no thorough understanding of commodity flows to inform the development of transport infrastructure to serve freight demand.

This chapter presents the first national freight demand analysis for Bangladesh. The analysis answers the following questions: How much freight is generated in Bangladesh? Where is freight being generated? Where is freight going? How is freight transported?

BANGLADESH'S TRANSPORT NETWORK

Bangladesh's complex network of national and regional highways and district (*zila*) roads totals more than 21,300 kilometers and includes more than 4,500 bridges over rivers. Bangladesh also has an estimated 304,380 kilometers of rural roads. Road density in Bangladesh is a mere 0.13 kilometers per 1,000 people for highways and district roads; including rural roads raises Bangladesh's figure to 1.9 kilometers per 1,000 people. These figures compare very poorly with road density in Pakistan (1.5 kilometers per 1,000 people), India (3.5), Sri Lanka (5.5) and Bhutan (9.7) (Andrés and others 2013).

Bangladesh Railway serves 44 of the country's 64 districts, with 2,877 kilometers of rail tracks. It connects with Indian Railway at several points, particularly on its west and northwest borders. Because of the riverine landscape, the network splits into east and west zones, with a single connection between the two. The railway network also has meter and broad gauges, which limits the smooth flow of passengers and cargo across the country.

Bangladesh's extensive river network of about 24,000 kilometers provides an alternative to land transport. About 6,000 kilometers are navigable in the monsoon season; just 3,800 kilometers can be navigated in the dry season. About 40 percent of the network is too shallow for large vessels, particularly in the northern part of the country.

FREIGHT GENERATION

Freight generation is the amount of cargo generated by an economic establishment, typically measured by weight or volume. It is a reflection of a production process in which intermediate inputs, land, labor, and capital interact to create economic outputs.

Two distinct processes generate cargo: the processes of incoming and outgoing cargo. Freight attraction is the amount of cargo brought to an establishment to be processed, stored, or sold to customers. Most establishments receive supplies and hence have positive freight attraction. Freight production is the amount of cargo sent out of the establishment for use at another establishment. Establishments that sell final products to consumers typically have zero freight production, whereas establishments that conduct intermediate processing activities have positive freight production. The freight generation of an establishment is the sum of its freight attraction and production.

A country's productive sectors can be classified as freight intensive or services intensive. Freight- intensive sectors are economic sectors for which the production and consumption of freight is an essential component of their economic activity. Services-intensive sectors are sectors in which the provision of services is the main activity. Nine sectors are classified as freight intensive and 10 as services intensive (table 2.1).

Freight transport and logistics are crucial to Bangladesh's economy. About 96 percent of establishments and 90 percent of employment are in freight-intensive sectors (table 2.2). In contrast, in metropolitan areas in the United States, these numbers are 45 percent and 50 percent, respectively (Holguín-Veras and others 2018). The heavy freight intensity of Bangladesh's economy means that transport and logistics systems directly affect most sectors and that inefficiencies in freight transport and logistics have a large impact on the economy.

How is freight generation estimated?

Four thousand economic establishments across the six largest freight-intensive sectors and across the country were surveyed. Freight-intensive sectors were the focus, because these sectors primarily determine freight dynamics. The survey collected data on characteristics of the establishments (economic sector, employment, land area, and so forth) similar to the data collected by the 2008 Agriculture Census, and 2013 Economic Census.[1] It also collected data on establishments' freight activities (volume of cargo in and out, number of freight vehicles in and out, mode share, and seasonal variations). Appendix A describes the sampling strategy and provides a copy of the survey.

TABLE 2.1 **Freight intensive and service intensive sectors**

TYPE OF SECTOR	SECTORS
Freight intensive	Agriculture
	Manufacturing
	Wholesale trade
	Retail trade and repair of motor vehicles
	Transport and storage
	Accommodation and food services
	Construction
	Mining and quarrying
	Electricity, gas, steam, air conditioning supply
	Water supply, sewerage, waste management
Services intensive	Information and communication activities
	Financial and insurance activities
	Real estate activities
	Professional, scientific, and technical activities
	Administrative and support service activities
	Public administration and defense
	Education
	Human health and social work activities
	Arts and entertainment
	Other

Source: Bangladesh Standard Industrial Classification.

TABLE 2.2 **Number of establishments and level of employment in Bangladesh, by sector**

SECTOR	ESTABLISHMENTS		EMPLOYMENT	
	NUMBER	PERCENT OF TOTAL	NUMBER	PERCENT OF TOTAL
Freight-intensive sectors				
Agriculture	28,695,763	78.22	29,661,026	54.72
Wholesale and retail	3,666,495	9.99	8,609,844	15.89
Transport and storage	1,337,631	3.65	1,921,893	3.55
Manufacturing	877,980	2.39	6,925,156	12.78
Accommodation and food services	531,324	1.45	1,233,264	2.28
Mining and quarrying	20,221	0.06	62,501	0.12
Construction	8,186	0.02	46,237	0.09
Electricity, gas, steam, air conditioning supply	3,727	0.01	56,231	0.10
Water supply, sewerage, waste management	2,452	0.01	14,172	0.03
Service-intensive sectors				
Other service activities	1,063,114	2.90	2,236,703	4.13
Education	192,986	0.53	1,489,955	2.75
Human health and social work activities	81,342	0.22	420,842	0.78
Administrative and support service activities	48,690	0.13	151,858	0.28
Financial and insurance activities	47,684	0.13	474,796	0.88
Professional, scientific, and technical activities	45,547	0.12	160,329	0.30
Public administration and defense	26,542	0.07	572,658	1.06
Information and communication activities	19,683	0.05	100,779	0.19
Art and entertainment	12,078	0.03	32,996	0.06
Real estate activities	5,398	0.01	29,045	0.05

Source: BBS 2010, 2013.

TABLE 2.3 **Distribution of freight attraction and production in sample**

KILOGRAMS/DAY	FREIGHT ATTRACTION		FREIGHT PRODUCTION	
	NUMBER OF OBSERVATIONS	PERCENT OF SAMPLE	NUMBER OF OBSERVATIONS	PERCENT OF SAMPLE
0–25	825	22	764	22
> 25–50	318	9	356	10
> 50–100	353	10	403	11
> 100–250	486	13	465	13
> 250–500	318	9	339	10
> 500–1,000	260	7	258	7
> 1,000–2,500	273	7	301	9
> 2,500–5,000	236	6	173	5
> 5,000–10,000	218	6	135	4
> 10,000	396	11	338	10
Total	3.683	100	3,532	100

Source: World Bank.

About 22 percent of the establishments surveyed receive 25 kilograms of cargo or less a day; 54 percent receive 250 kilograms a day or less (table 2.3). The remaining establishments are distributed almost uniformly between the ranges of cargo attracted. About 56 percent of establishments ship less than 250 kilograms a day. The average weight of cargo attracted and produced for all sectors are almost equal at 8,965 and 8,963 kilograms a day, with standard deviations of 38,713 and 46,033 kilograms a day, respectively.

Econometric models of freight attraction and production were estimated using the survey data.[2] Research by Holguín-Veras and others (2011, 2013, 2014, 2016) and Holguín-Veras and Gonzalez-Calderon (2016) indicates that it is usually best to use employment and other economic indicators, such as firm sales, as independent variables in the estimation of freight generation models. Freight attraction and production models using employment as the independent variable were estimated at the two-digit Bangladesh Standard Industrial Classification (BSIC) level to capture the variability inherent to each industry, as represented by equation (2.1). As the intent of the analysis is to understand patterns of inter-district freight flows, the models were estimated using only freight that travels more than one hour.

$$FG_i = f_n \text{ (Employment}_i) \qquad (2.1)$$

where FG = freight generation, i = establishment, and n = sector. Different functional forms were considered, given the inherent heterogeneity of freight generation patterns across sectors and the lack of larger sets of explanatory variables because of data limitations. Certain industry sectors display a constant rate of cargo generated, whereas others may increase their rate of cargo generation proportionally to employment, as Holguín-Veras and others (2016) show. An assumption that only one functional form is applicable across all economic sectors could lead to serious errors in the estimation of cargo generated.

Four functional forms were considered. The first type of model is linear. It estimates the amount of cargo generated as the product of employment times a parameter that captures the proportion at which changes in employment increase or decrease the amount of cargo generated. The other three types of models—linear-logarithmic, exponential, and power models—can capture nonlinear patterns in the data (appendix B briefly describes the four models).

The results from the most significant models were applied to data from the 2008 Agriculture Census and the 2013 Economic Census for establishments with more than two employees, to estimate inter-district freight generation for every district in Bangladesh.[3] Appendix C presents the estimation results for the most significant models. The results from the two-digit BSIC level estimations were aggregated into six sectors: agriculture, manufacturing, wholesale, retail, transport, and food.

Where is freight generated in Bangladesh?

Bangladesh generates about 470,000 tons of inter-district freight (3.3 kilograms per capita) a day from freight-intensive sectors of the economy.[4] Manufacturing accounts for the largest share of inter-district freight generated (53 percent), followed by agriculture (25 percent), wholesale (12 percent), retail (8 percent), and transport and storage and accommodation and food services (1 percent each).

Freight generation by district

Freight generation in Bangladesh is highly concentrated in a few districts. The top 10 generate 42 percent of all inter-district freight, the 11th–20th districts generate only 20 percent, and the bottom 10 districts generate less than 5 percent. Dhaka and Chattogram districts, where the two largest cities in the country are located and a significant share of manufacturing takes place, are the top two districts, generating 13 percent and 6 percent of all inter-district freight in the country, respectively.[5] The top 10 districts are along the northwest–southeast corridor; 7 of the top 10 are east of the Padma and Brahmaputra rivers (map 2.1). In the northwest, only Rangpur, Bogura, and Sirajhanj districts are among the top 10 in inter-district freight generated.

Dhaka is also the top district in terms of inter-district freight generation per capita. It is not as far from the other districts, however (figure 2.1). Dhaka generates 8.2 kilograms per person per day, followed by Rangpur (7.9) and Gazipur (7.8). Chattogram drops to the middle of the ranking in per capita terms, largely because the freight generated at Chattogram Port is not accounted for in the estimations. Inter-district freight generated per capita in Dhaka is three times the inter-district freight generated per capita in Coxsbazar (the district with the lowest freight generation per capita) and 1.05 times that of Rangpur. In comparison, inter-district freight generated in Dhaka is 43 times the inter-district freight generated in Jhalokati (the district with the lowest freight generation) and 2.3 times that of Chattogram. The differences between the spatial distributions of total freight generation and freight generation per capita reflect different sectoral compositions, the share of micro-establishments, and the share of the working population.

Dhaka is the economic center of Bangladesh, accounting for 10 percent of the country's population and more than a third of its urban population.

MAP 2.1

Inter-district freight generated in Bangladesh, by district

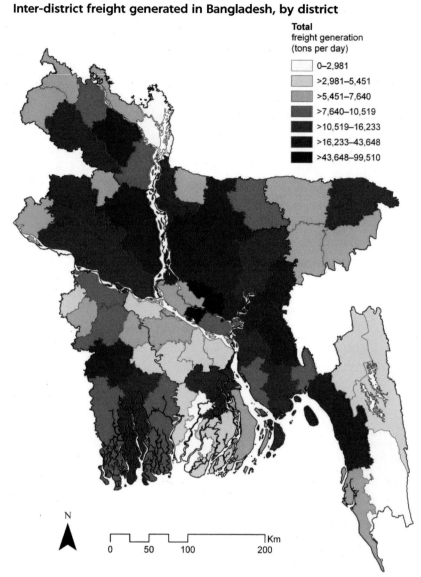

Total
freight generation
(tons per day)

☐	0–2,981
☐	>2,981–5,451
☐	>5,451–7,640
☐	>7,640–10,519
☐	>10,519–16,233
☐	>16,233–43,648
☐	>43,648–99,510

Source: World Bank analysis.

Greater Dhaka generates 20 percent of the country's GDP and almost half its formal employment (Bird and others 2018). Dhaka district generates the most inter-district freight of all the districts in Bangladesh. On average, the shorter a district's travel time to Dhaka, the more inter-district freight it generates (figure 2.2), highlighting the centrality of Dhaka.

Freight generation by sector

Manufacturing generates the most inter-district freight in 53 districts; it is also concentrated in a few districts. In Munshiganj, Gazipur, and Narayanganj districts, manufacturing generates more than 75 percent of inter-district freight. In Dhaka district, it accounts for 54 percent. Dhaka district and *upazilas* in Gazipur, Narayanganj, and Narsingdi districts form the Greater Dhaka metropolitan area, the most important manufacturing center in the country.

FIGURE 2.1

Per capita inter-district freight generation in Bangladesh, by district

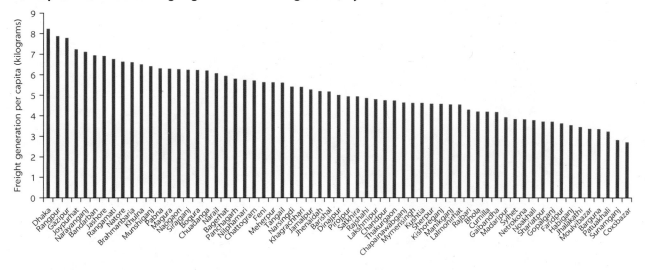

Source: World Bank analysis.

FIGURE 2.2

Correlation between freight generation and distance to Dhaka

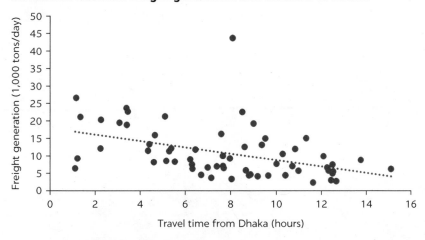

Source: World Bank analysis.
Note: Travel time is based on travel by road, using speed data collected by the authors.
The outlier is Chattogram district, home to the country's largest sea port.

Dhaka, Gazipur, and Narayanganj districts generate 22 percent of Bangladesh's manufacturing inter-district freight. Ten districts generate 46 percent of inter-district freight generated by manufacturing; 6 of them are east of the Padma and Brahmaputra rivers (map 2.2).

Agriculture generates the most inter-district freight in only 10 districts. It is less concentrated than manufacturing freight generation. In Barguna, Lalmonirhat, Habiganj, and Kishoreganj districts, agriculture generates more than 50 percent of inter-district freight. Cumilla district generates about 9,200 tons a day of agricultural inter-district freight, more than any other district; it accounts for 4.8 percent of agriculture inter-district freight in the country. Mymensingh and Jamalpur districts in Mymensingh division,

MAP 2.2

Inter-district freight generated in Bangladesh, by sector and district

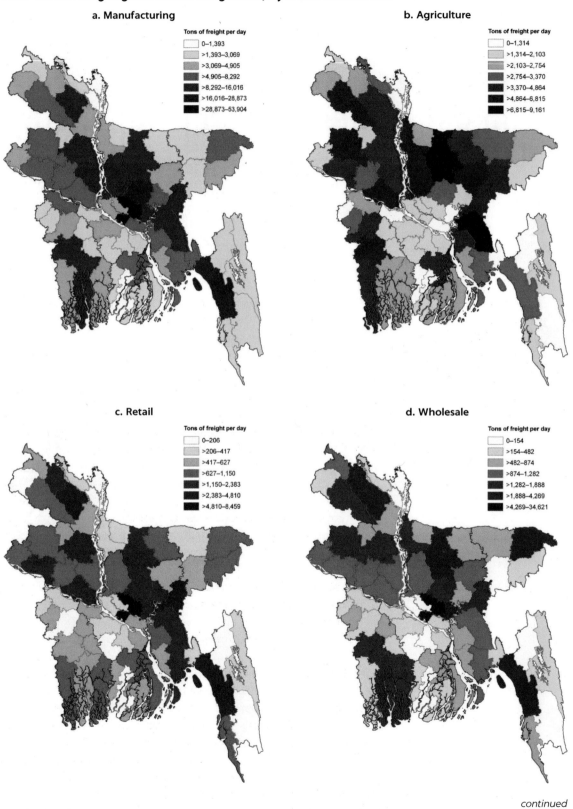

a. Manufacturing

Tons of freight per day
- 0–1,393
- >1,393–3,069
- >3,069–4,905
- >4,905–8,292
- >8,292–16,016
- >16,016–28,873
- >28,873–53,904

b. Agriculture

Tons of freight per day
- 0–1,314
- >1,314–2,103
- >2,103–2,754
- >2,754–3,370
- >3,370–4,864
- >4,864–6,815
- >6,815–9,161

c. Retail

Tons of freight per day
- 0–206
- >206–417
- >417–627
- >627–1,150
- >1,150–2,383
- >2,383–4,810
- >4,810–8,459

d. Wholesale

Tons of freight per day
- 0–154
- >154–482
- >482–874
- >874–1,282
- >1,282–1,888
- >1,888–4,269
- >4,269–34,621

continued

MAP 2.2, *continued*

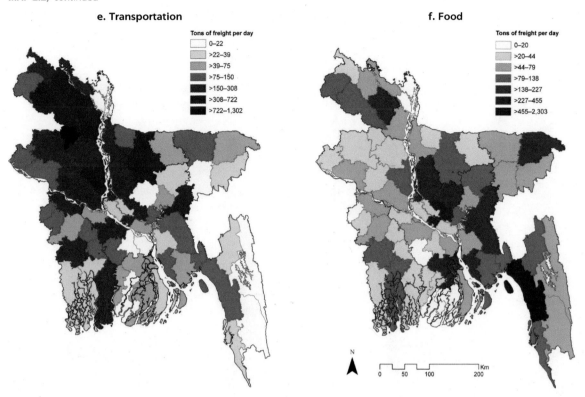

Source: World Bank analysis.

Kishoreganj district in Dhaka division, and Dinajpur district in Rangpur division complete the top five generators of agricultural inter-district freight. About 32 percent of inter-district freight generated by agriculture is generated in the top 10 districts, 5 of which are west of the Padma and Brahmaputra rivers (map 2.2).

Inter-district freight generation is more concentrated in Dhaka in the wholesale sector than the retail sector. Dhaka district generates 37 percent of inter-district freight in the wholesale sector, followed by Chattogram, with 5 percent. The top 10 districts generate 62 percent of inter-district freight in the wholesale sector, making it the most concentrated sector in terms of freight generation. Dhaka (14 percent), Chattogram (8 percent), and Rangpur (6 percent) generate the most inter-district freight from the retail sector. The top 10 districts generate 48 percent of retail inter-district freight; 6 of them are east of the Padma and Brahmaputra rivers.

Inter-district freight generation in the transport sector is concentrated in the west of the country. Joypurhat district in Rajshahi division accounts for about 14 percent of inter-district freight in the sector, followed by Rangpur (8 percent) and Gaibandha (6 percent) districts in Rangpur division. The top 10 districts generate 51 percent of inter-district freight in the transport sector; 8 of them are west of the Padma and Brahmaputra rivers.

The food service sector is the second-most concentrated in terms of inter-district freight generation. Chattogram district generates 32 percent of inter-district freight, followed by Dhaka, with 6 percent. The top 10 districts generate 59 percent of inter-district freight in the food service sector; 7 of them are the east of the Padma and Brahmaputra rivers.

FREIGHT MOVEMENT BY ROAD

Bangladesh's road network carries a high level of traffic. Average annual daily traffic exceeded 20,000 vehicles in some locations in 2013.[6] Traffic is highly concentrated in and around Dhaka and Chattogram.

Freight vehicles account for 18 percent of national traffic, 19 percent of inter-district traffic, and 16 percent of urban traffic. They are highly concentrated in and around Dhaka. The concentration of freight vehicle traffic is also heavy along the Dhaka–Chattogram corridor. The Dhaka–northwest corridor has relatively high volume of truck-based traffic, followed by the Dhaka–northeast and the Dhaka–southwest corridors.

The most prevalent form of freight vehicle in Bangladesh is medium trucks. Different freight vehicle types generally perform different functions. Heavy and medium trucks are used mainly for long-haul deliveries; small and utility trucks are used for short-haul or local deliveries. Medium trucks account for 54 percent of all freight vehicle traffic volume, followed by small trucks (33 percent), utility trucks (9 percent), and heavy trucks (3 percent).

Bangladesh has a small share of heavy trucks. In 1982 the Dominican Republic—a country that is much smaller than Bangladesh, with a per capita income in 1982 comparable to that of Bangladesh in 2018—had a much larger share of heavy trucks (8 percent) and a smaller share of medium trucks (34 percent) than Bangladesh (Holguín-Veras 1984).

Most small and utility truck traffic is around urban areas, with a concentration in Dhaka (map 2.3). Heavy trucks are found along the Dhaka–Chattogram and Dhaka–Sylhet corridors, with a concentration in and around Chattogram. Medium trucks are distributed throughout the country. The nature of traffic within and outside urban areas differs. More intra-city, short-haul trips take place in urban areas, and more inter-district, long-haul trips take place outside urban areas, explaining the differences in traffic of different truck sizes.

How is freight movement on roads estimated?

What is the origin and destination of trucks making inter-district trips? Unlike the United States, Colombia, and other countries, Bangladesh does not undertake a commodity flow survey. There is therefore no origin-destination matrix for freight in Bangladesh. This section describes a modeling approach that uses the freight generation estimated in previous sections and the actual freight traffic on the roads to produce an origin-destination matrix for cargo transported by road.

Holguín-Veras and Patil (2007, 2008) developed the freight origin-destination synthesis (FODS) model, which estimates the freight origin-destination matrixes that best replicate actual truck traffic on the roads. The FODS considers only trips from a single origin to a single destination, which tends to be the pattern of inter-district freight traffic.

The FODS uses a demand model based on gravity equations to estimate the flows between origins and destinations. It estimates the parameters of the demand model so that the resulting traffic flows resemble the observed traffic in the network. It assigns total truck trips to the network to obtain a set of estimated truck traffic volumes, which are compared with observed truck traffic.

The FODS considers both loaded and empty trips. The inclusion of empty trips is very important, because a significant number of empty trucks ply the roads. Failing to account for empty trips produces large errors in the estimation

MAP 2.3

Volume of truck traffic in Bangladesh (vehicles per day) 2013, by type of truck

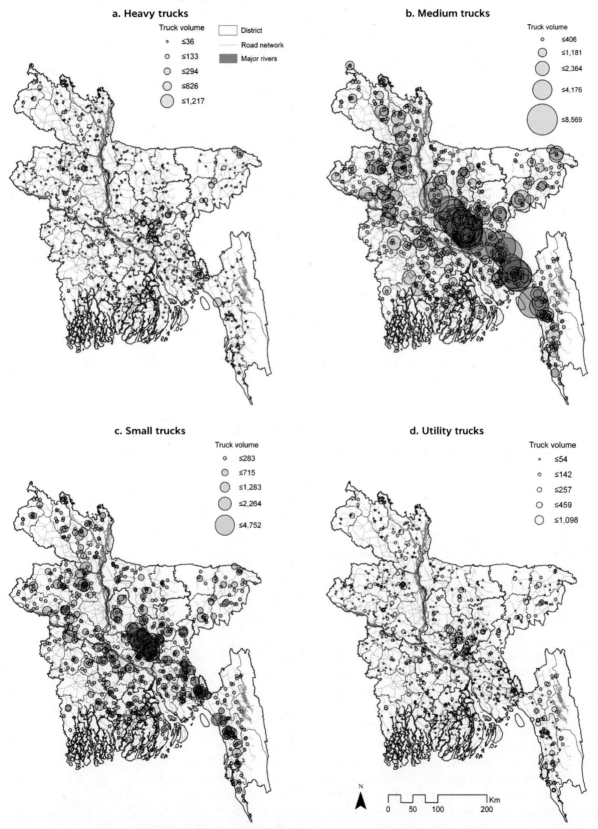

a. Heavy trucks

Truck volume
- ≤36
- ≤133
- ≤294
- ≤626
- ≤1,217

District
Road network
Major rivers

b. Medium trucks

Truck volume
- ≤406
- ≤1,181
- ≤2,364
- ≤4,176
- ≤8,569

c. Small trucks

Truck volume
- ≤283
- ≤715
- ≤1,283
- ≤2,264
- ≤4,752

d. Utility trucks

Truck volume
- ≤54
- ≤142
- ≤257
- ≤459
- ≤1,098

N

Km
0   50   100   200

Source: World Bank, using data from the Bangladesh Road and Highways Department.

of directional traffic, as Holguín-Veras and Thorson (2003) note. The FODS uses the model originally formulated by Noortman and Van Es (1978), which considers the probability of empty return trips.

There are two types of FODS. A single-commodity FODS estimates a single gravity model and the share of empty trips for all commodities together. A multicommodity FODS estimates a gravity model for each commodity separately and estimates an average share of empty trips for the total cargo. The multicommodity FODS could also be thought of as a multisector FODS, as the FODS models the bundle of commodities produced and consumed by a freight-intensive sector without attempting to model specific commodities.

The freight flows between Bangladesh's land ports, seaports, and airports and the rest of the country represent the movement of import and export cargo. As the FODS focuses on the domestic transport of freight, flows to and from ports must be removed from the traffic counts.[7] It makes sense to estimate the traffic imports and exports generate in the network using import and export data. The traffic flows between ports and districts are estimated based on gravity equations for exports and imports. Appendix D presents a technical description of the FODS and port of entry/exit models.

Where is freight moving on roads?

This section presents the estimated matrix of origin-destinations for road-based inter-district freight from agriculture, manufacturing, retail, wholesale, transport, and food services.

FIGURE 2.3

Freight origin-destination matrix for international and domestic inter-district road traffic in Bangladesh

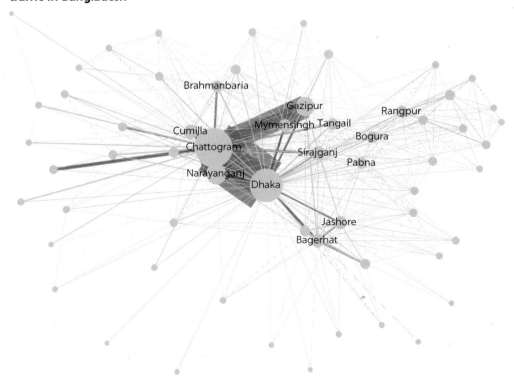

Source: World Bank analysis.
Note: The orange lines represent the 14 largest freight flows between pairs of districts.

Chattogram is central to the movement of international (imports and exports) and domestic inter-district freight in Bangladesh. Figure 2.3 depicts the international and domestic flows between pairs of districts. The thickness of a link between two districts represents the total volume of freight flowing in both directions. The three thickest links are between Chattogram and Dhaka, Narayanganj, and Gazipur districts. Chattogram Port handles more than 80 percent of all international trade by weight. Dhaka, Gazipur, and Narayanganj are part of Greater Dhaka, the country's main economic center. These patterns of economic activity and trade reveal the importance of Chattogram district in the movement of inter-district freight and the importance of its links with Dhaka, Narayanganj, and Gazipur districts.

Dhaka is central to the movement of domestic inter-district freight. The three thickest links in figure 2.4, which depicts domestic flows between pairs of districts, are between Dhaka district and Chattogram, Narayanganj, and Mymensingh districts. It is estimated that about 3,500 medium truck equivalents (MTEs) enter and exit Dhaka district per day carrying domestic inter-district freight from the agriculture, manufacturing, retail, wholesale, transport, and food sectors.[8] The top three destinations for freight originating in Dhaka are Chattogram (202 MTE per day),[9] Narayanganj (190), and Sirajganj (135) districts. The top three districts that send freight to Dhaka district are Chattogram (223 MTE per day),[10] Narayanganj (176), and Mymensingh (153).

Once Dhaka district is removed from the picture, the thickest links for most districts tend to be with neighboring districts. Rangpur's largest inter-district freight flows outside Dhaka are with two of its neighboring districts, Dinajpur and Nilphamari. Khulna's thickest links outside Dhaka are with Jeshore and

FIGURE 2.4

Freight origin-destination matrix for domestic inter-district road traffic in Bangladesh

Source: World Bank analysis.
Note: The orange lines represent the 14 largest freight flows between pairs of districts.

Satkhira districts. Sylhet's thickest link outside Dhaka is with Sunamganj, a neighboring district. Gazipur's thickest links outside Dhaka are with Mymensingh, a neighboring district, and Sirajganj, a close-by district. Even Chattogram's linkage with the rest of the country in terms of domestic inter-district freight is surprisingly local once Dhaka is removed from the picture. Chattogram's thickest links outside Dhaka are with Cumilla and Coxsbazar districts.

Dhaka's importance in the movement of inter-district freight is driven primarily by the manufacturing and wholesale sectors and to some extent by the retail sector. Dhaka district generates the most freight from manufacturing, wholesale and retail sectors, so the thickest links in all three sectors are between Dhaka and other districts (figure 2.5). For manufacturing and wholesale, the thickest links are between Dhaka and Chattogram, Mymensingh, and Narayanganj. For retail the thickest links are between Dhaka and Chattogram, Mymensingh, and Cumilla.

For agriculture, the sector that generates the second-largest amount of freight, there is no district that is as important as Dhaka is in other sectors. The thickest links are between Mymensingh and Kishoreganj and Jamalpur districts, followed by the Rangpur–Dinajpur and Mymensingh–Netrokona links (figure 2.6). Cumilla–Kishoreganj is the fifth-thickest link, and Cumilla is the district with the largest generation of freight in the agriculture sector.

FIGURE 2.5

Freight origin-destination matrix for road traffic in Bangladesh from the manufacturing and food sectors

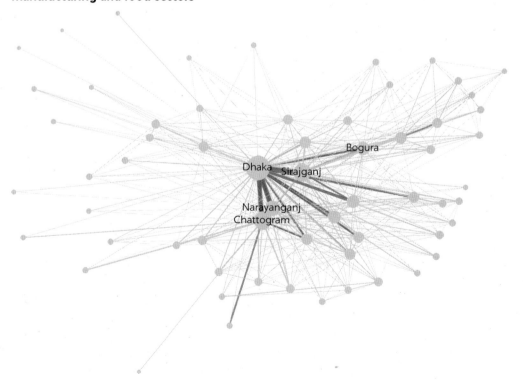

Source: World Bank analysis.
Note: The orange lines represent the 14 largest freight flows between pairs of districts.

FIGURE 2.6

Freight origin-destination matrix for road traffic in Bangladesh from agriculture

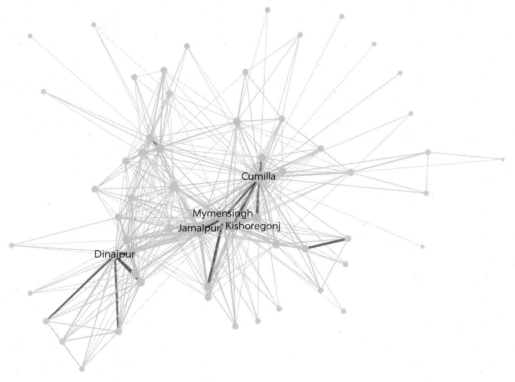

Source: World Bank analysis.
Note: The orange lines represent the 14 largest freight flows between pairs of districts.

Understanding how freight flows through the road network, and which roads are highly demanded by trucks, is critical for planning transport infrastructure development. As the road network, particularly the primary network, is sparse in Bangladesh, trucks carrying freight from different origin-destination pairs must share the same roads.

The northwest–southeast corridor, traversing the country from Rangpur division to Chattogram division, is Bangladesh's backbone. Total inter-district freight demand is highest in the Dhaka–Chattogram section (map 2.4). For domestic inter-district freight only, demand is highest in the Dhaka–Sirajganj section (map 2.5). The Dhaka–Chattogram section connects the largest city in the country with the second-largest city and main seaport, which handles more than 90 percent of seaborne trade. The Dhaka–Sirajganj section connects Dhaka (and Chattogram) with the west of Bangladesh through the Bangabandhu Bridge, the only bridge connecting the east and west of the country. The ferries crossing the Padma River that connect the southwest with Dhaka and other divisions in the east are inefficient, with long and uncertain waiting times. A large number of trucks thus take the longer route across the Bangabandhu Bridge to reach the southwest districts and the border with India.

Freight demand in the northeast–southwest corridors and the north–south corridor connecting Khulna and Rajshahi divisions in the west

MAP 2.4

International and domestic inter-district freight flows in Bangladesh

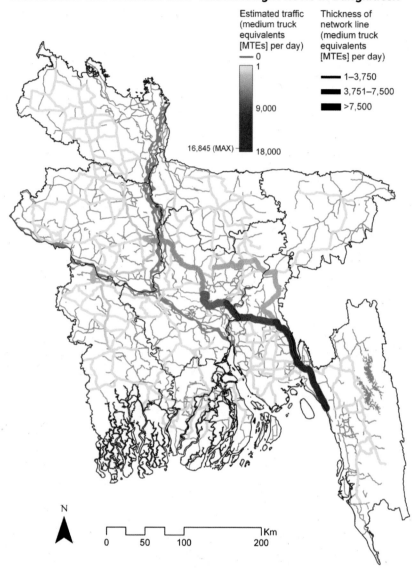

Estimated traffic
(medium truck
equivalents
[MTEs] per day)
— 0
1
9,000
16,845 (MAX) — 18,000

Thickness of
network line
(medium truck
equivalents
[MTEs] per day)
— 1–3,750
— 3,751–7,500
— >7,500

N

Km
0   50   100   200

Source: World Bank analysis.

is medium. Two distinct sections can be identified along the northeast-southwest corridor: the Dhaka–Sylhet section and Dhaka–southwest section via the Mawa–Kaorakandi ferry. Freight demand on the latter section comes from trucks that prefer to cross the Padma River using ferries than take the longer-distance route across the Bangabandhu Bridge. Some of these trucks deal with the long waiting times at ferry crossings by making payments to facilitate preferential boarding.

Freight demand for inter-district roads hides an important inefficiency in the trucking sector—the fact that 35 percent of all inter-district truck trips run empty. Chapters 4 and 5 discuss the reasons for the high level of empty trips. Some of the most important reasons include the high concentration of economic activity in Dhaka and Chattogram and inefficiencies in the market for trucking services, which cause many shippers to own their own fleets of trucks to transport only their own cargo.

MAP 2.5

Domestic inter-district freight flows in Bangladesh

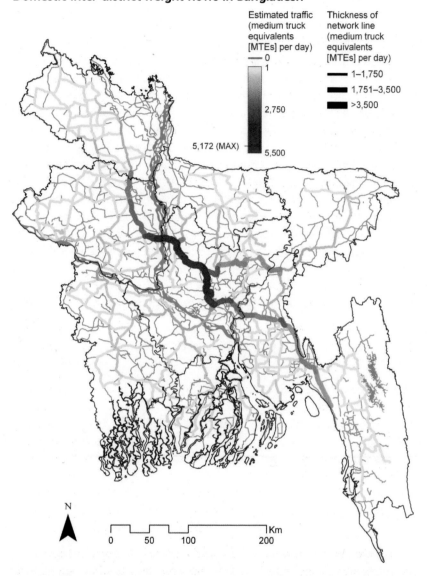

Source: World Bank analysis.

FREIGHT MOVEMENT BY INLAND WATERWAY

About 30 inland river ports are located across the country. Twelve of them handle most of Bangladesh's cargo, playing an important role in the movement of cargo across the country. The river ports are interconnected through Class I–III waterways.[11] They provide about 800 landing stations and are directly connected with the Chattogram and Mongla seaports. All inland river ports are the responsibility of the Bangladesh Inland Waterway Transport Authority (BIWTA). In some cases, BIWTA concessions the operation to private players on an annual basis. Several shared or dedicated facilities have been developed by the private sector.

The inland waterway transport network and the ports handling cargo can be divided into five regions (map 2.6).

MAP 2.6

Main river ports in Bangladesh

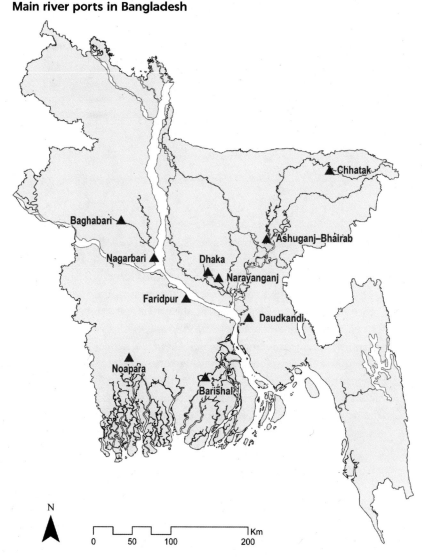

Source: World Bank analysis.

1. Dhaka region (Dhaka, Narayanganj, Munshiganj, Narsingdi, and Gazipur districts): The ports of Dhaka and Narayanganj, with multiple handling locations at Gabtoli, Aliganj, Pagla, Fatullah, and Kanchpur, and the Pangaon container terminal, handle freight demand in this region.

2. Northwest region: The ports of Baghabari and Nagarbari handle freight demand in this region, because the Jamuna River has very little draft north of the Nagarbari port region. As a result, no other ports farther north service the region.

3. Southwest region: The ports of Faridpur and Noapara and the private jetties in Khulna district handle freight demand in this region. The Faridpur Port serves Faridpur and Gopalganj districts; the Noapara Port and the private jetties in Khulna service the freight demand of the entire Khulna division.

4. Southeast region: The Barishal and Daudkandi ports and private jetties in Chattogram handle freight demand in this region. Barishal Port serves primarily the Barishal division, which includes all the southern regions, where there is little road connectivity. The Daudkandi Port serves Cumilla and parts of Feni district. Private jetties in Chattogram serve Chattogram district.

5. Northeast region: The Ashuganj–Bhairab and Chhatak ports handle freight demand in this region.

The inland waterway transport fleet comprises more than 11,000 vessels.[12] About 65 percent of the vessels are cargo vessels, including oil tankers, dumb barges, and sand carriers, with the latter the most common. The type, number, and capacity of vessels operating on each route are not available.

Infrastructure planning requires identifying the main river ports that generate freight demand and the main freight corridors along which freight moves. Understanding freight flow enables targeted interventions to be made in specific corridors to bring about transformational changes. Responsibility for maintaining the freight flow data on the inland water transport sector rests with the Bangladesh Inland Water Authority (BIWTA). However, BIWTA has no mechanism to accurately record freight flow movement. The data it records lack granularity by commodity and origin-destination flows and are not considered accurate or detailed enough to base actions on. Several studies on inland waterways have been conducted in Bangladesh, but none of them undertook a freight flow analysis.

How is freight movement on waterways estimated?

Freight flows on inland waterways were estimated based on the following types of primary and secondary data collected through interactions with stakeholders:

- primary visits to key river ports, to understand the different commodities handled at the port, cargo-handling mechanisms (manual versus mechanized), productivity levels, and the quantity and origin-destination patterns of commodities
- interactions with users of inland waterways transport, to identify and map their cargo movement
- interactions with other stakeholders, such as barge owners, labor contractors, commodities traders, and BIWTA officials, to confirm the understanding obtained through other interactions.

The total volume of a commodity handled at a port was estimated based on the monthly quantity handled at a jetty, the number of jetties handling the commodity at the port, and the seasonality of the commodity flows (equation 2.2). The monthly quantity loaded and unloaded at a jetty was determined based on the number of barges at the jetty and the average capacity of barges carrying the commodity. Based on these two factors, the analysis estimated the quantity of cargo loaded and unloaded per month and then annualized it by factoring in the seasonality of each commodity. For export and import commodities, the seasonality factor was calculated based on monthly import data of major commodities handled at Chattogram and Mongla ports during fiscal 2017. For domestic cargo, the seasonality factor was derived from primary interactions at river ports and industries.

$$\begin{array}{c} \text{Quantity} \\ \text{handled at} \\ \text{one jetty per} \\ \text{day per month} \end{array} \times \begin{array}{c} \text{Number of} \\ \text{jetties/handling} \\ \text{points} \end{array} \times \begin{array}{c} \text{Annualized} \\ \text{seasonality} \\ \text{factor} \end{array} = \begin{array}{c} \text{Total} \\ \text{volume of a} \\ \text{particular} \\ \text{commodity} \\ \text{handled at} \\ \text{port} \end{array} \qquad (2.2)$$

Several industries, such as cement, edible oil, and sugar, are located close to the river bank and have their own jetties for importing raw materials and dispatching finished goods. The quantity and origin destination pattern of commodities handled at these private jetties was estimated based on a combination of primary interactions and secondary research to assess the raw material requirements of the factory based on capacity and actual production figures. The import quantity of raw material was then distributed among the private jetties based on their capacity/production share:

$$\text{Total raw material imports} \times \text{Capacity in the region/total capacity} = \text{Total import at private jetties in the region} \qquad (2.3)$$

Estimates of freight production (loaded vessels) and freight attraction (unloaded vessels) were used to arrive at the freight origin-destination matrix at river ports. Commodities at river ports are either imported or domestic commodities. Imported commodities come from the Chattogram and Mongla ports and from India, through the Indo–Bangla protocol route. The aggregate results from equation (2.3) yielded the origin-destination flows for import commodities. The movement of export commodities is negligible, so it is not included in the analysis. In the case of flows of domestic commodities that originate from a single location, the loaded and unloaded estimates following equation (2.2) determined the flows to the different destinations. For domestic commodities with several origins and destinations across the country, the loaded and unloaded estimates from equation (2.2) were triangulated with information captured from interactions with stakeholders to determine each origin-destination pair.

How much greight is moving through inland waterways and where is it going?

About 76 million tons of cargo a year are transported through Bangladesh's inland water network, of which about 61 percent are imports. Clinker (the stony residue from burned coal or a furnace), fertilizer, and wheat constitute two-thirds of import movements on the inland water transport network (figure 2.7). The remaining third are coal; fly ash (ash produced in small dark flecks, typically from a furnace); sugar; edible oil; and other bulk commodities, including salt, steel scrap, ceramic sand, gypsum, and stones. Container movements are negligible, at 140,000 tons in 2017, almost all imports. Domestic freight flows on the inland water network are limited to construction materials, cement, petroleum products, and fertilizer (figure 2.8).[13] Construction materials include primarily sand and stones, which are mixed with cement to manufacture concrete.

About 79 percent of import flows on the inland water network are generated in Chattogram Port, 15 percent in Mongla Port, and 6 percent in Kolkata (India). During fiscal year 2017, Chattogram Port handled 73 million tons of imports, with about 36 million tons leaving the port on inland water vessels. The main destination of imports from Chattogram Port are ports in the Dhaka region (27 million tons), followed by private jetties in the Chattogram area (7 million tons). The southwest region, particularly Nagarbari Port, with 1.5 million tons, is the third most important destination of imports from Chattogram, followed by the northeast and southwest, with less than 1 million tons each. Mongla Port

FIGURE 2.7

Imported commodities transported on Bangladesh's inland water transport network

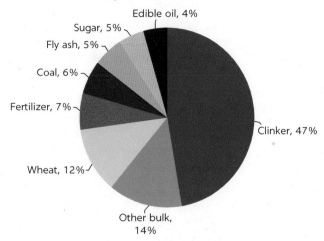

Source: PwC 2018.

FIGURE 2.8

Domestically produced commodities transported on Bangladesh's inland water transport network

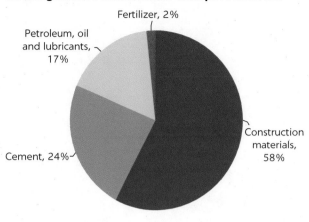

Source: PwC 2018.

handled 7.2 million tons of imports during fiscal year 2017, 96 percent of them transported to the southwest and southeast regions through the inland water transit network. The destinations of imports from Mongla Port are the private jetties in Khulna (3.7 million tons a year), Noapara Port (2.9 million tons), and Barishal Port (0.2 million tons). Of the 2.6 million tons of cargo originating in Kolkata during fiscal year 2017, 96 percent went to the Dhaka region and the rest to Mongla Port.

Five regions are key locations for all freight trips on inland waterways in Bangladesh (maps 2.7 and 2.8). The Chattogram region generates 41.9 million tons a year, consisting of cargo from Chattogram Port, the Karnaphuli fertilizer factory in Chattogram, and the main storage depots of oil companies. This cargo comprises all major import commodities and domestically produced fertilizer and petroleum products, which are handled at various river ports and private jetties. The Mongla region generates about 7 million tons a year, consisting of cargo from Mongla Port and the private jetty of cement companies in Mongla. Coal, fertilizer, clinker, and cement are the key commodities. The Kolkata region generates 2.4 million tons a year of fly ash, which is carried through the Indo–Bangla route and consumed by cement companies in Narayanganj and Khulna. The Dhaka–Narayanganj region generates 5.9 million tons a year, consisting primarily of cement cargo originating from the private jetties of cement factories and fertilizer (0.1 million tons a year) from the Ashuganj fertilizer factory. The Sylhet region generates about 18.4 million tons a year, consisting of construction materials and cement. Ten river ports handle 86 percent of cargo (figure 2.9).

Freight flows of key commodities

Clinker, fly ash, and cement flows

Flows of clinker, fly ash, and cement are related, as factories import clinker and fly ash to produce cement. As all the major cement factories in Bangladesh are located along rivers, it is convenient for them to import raw materials to their own jetties. The largest cement production clusters are in the Dhaka region, with about

MAP 2.7

Freight flows of imported goods on inland waterways in Bangladesh

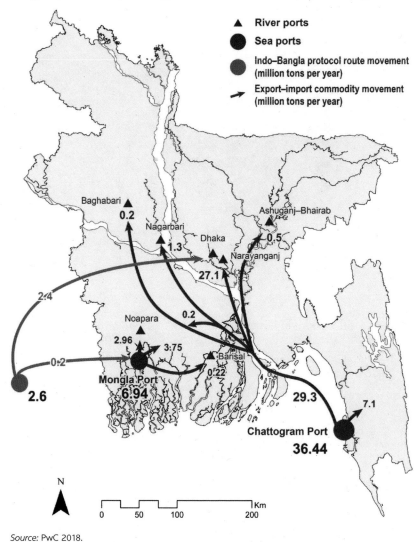

Source: PwC 2018.

65 percent of national production capacity, Chattogram (18 percent of capacity), the Khulna area (10 percent), and the Sylhet region (4 percent) follow.

Factories in the Dhaka region import clinker through Chattogram Port. Factories in western Bangladesh import it through Mongla Port. In fiscal year 2017, about 20 million tons of clinker were imported at Chattogram Port and about 2 million tons at Mongla Port. About 80 percent of clinker imported through Chattogram is transported on barges through inland waterways to factory jetties in the Dhaka region. The remaining 20 percent is transported on barges to the factory jetties in Chattogram. The clinker imported at Mongla Port is transported to the cement factory jetties in the Khulna area.

Fly ash is imported through the Indo–Bangla protocol routes and handled at the private jetties of cement companies in Khulna and Dhaka region. Of the 2.5 million tons imported in fiscal year 2017, 92 percent is destined for private jetties in the Dhaka region. The rest is imported at Mongla Port and then distributed to private jetties in the Khulna region.[14]

Flows of cement on inland waterways (of about 7 million tons a year) originate primarily in the Dhaka region, followed by the Sylhet region and a very small

MAP 2.8

Freight flows of domestically produced goods on inland waterways in Bangladesh

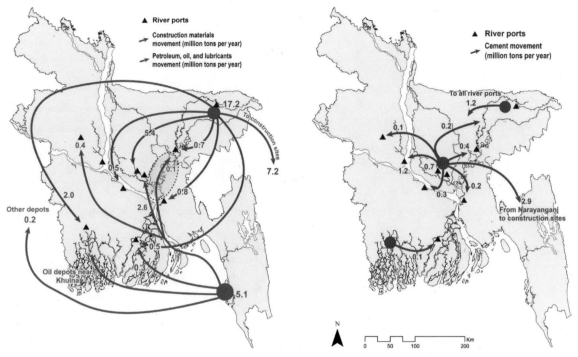

Source: PwC 2018.

FIGURE 2.9

Distribution of inland water traffic in Bangladesh, by river port

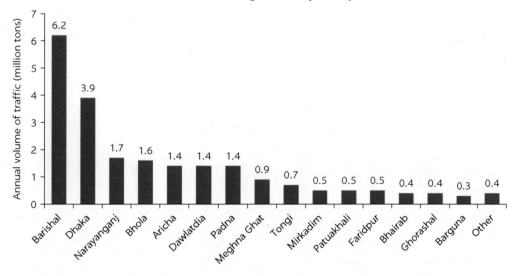

Source: PwC 2018.

quantity in the Khulna area. About 30 percent of cement is shipped via the inland waterway network. The share is larger in the Khulna and Sylhet regions, with factories in Sylhet dispatching 80 percent of their finished product through inland waterways. Demand for cement in Southern Bangladesh, particularly Chattogram, is almost entirely served by the factories in Dhaka region and Chattogram, which transport it by road. The main destinations of the cement flows on inland waterways are in the Dhaka region, the northwest region, and sites of large construction projects across the country, such as the Padma Bridge (map 2.9). Flows to construction projects last only for the duration of the projects.

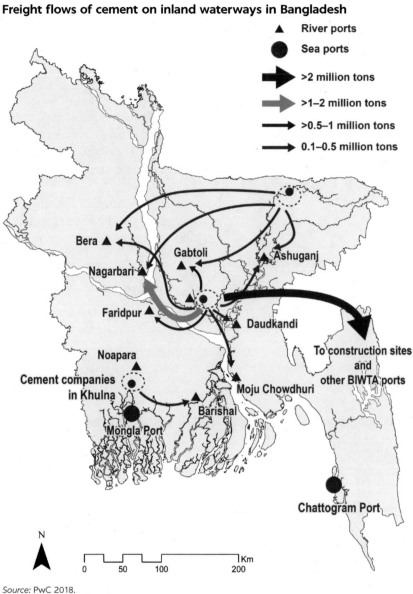

MAP 2.9

MAP 2.9

Freight flows of cement on inland waterways in Bangladesh

Source: PwC 2018.

Fertilizer

Bangladesh's meets its annual demand for fertilizer of about 4 million tons of fertilizer through domestic production and imports. The Bangladesh Chemical Industries Corporation (BCIC) produces urea-based fertilizer. Because natural gas is not readily available in Bangladesh, domestic production is limited to 0.7–1 million tons a year, which varies per gas availability. The balance is met through imports. The government controls the import and distribution of fertilizer through the National Fertilizer Distribution Co-ordination Committee, under the Ministry of Agriculture, which assesses regional fertilizer demand and distributes import requirements of urea to BCIC and non-urea imports to the Bangladesh Agricultural Development Corporation (BADC) and private sector importers.

About 3.5 million tons of fertilizer is transported along the country's inland waterways per year. Bangladesh imported about 3 million tons of fertilizer in fiscal year 2017, distributed evenly between Mongla and Chattogram ports, for distribution to various regions. The imported fertilizer is distributed to different buffer warehouses of the BCIC and BADC through inland waterways to river ports, particularly Baghabari, Nagarbari and Noapara (map 2.10). Domestically produced fertilizer is also transported through inland waterways, mainly from Chattogram to Baghabari and Nagarbari ports in the northwest.

Wheat

Demand for wheat in Bangladesh more than doubled between 2013 and 2017, from 3 million to 7 million tons, thanks to the shift in consumption from rice toward wheat (USDA 2017). Domestic production of wheat is only 1.5 million tons a year; the balance is met through imports. Bangladesh imported about 5.5 million tons of wheat through the ports of Chattogram (5.1 million tons) and Mongla (0.4 million tons) in fiscal 2017.

An estimated 4 million tons a year of wheat is dispatched through inland waterways from Chattogram to the Narayanganj region, where a cluster of wheat flour mills are located. The remaining 1 million tons is consumed within the

MAP 2.10

Freight flows of fertilizer on inland waterways in Bangladesh

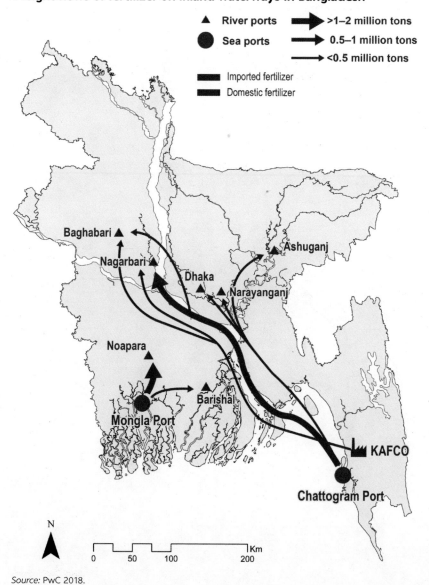

Source: PwC 2018.

Chattogram region (map 2.11). The wheat imported at Mongla Port primarily meets demand by the Khulna region; it is handled at Noapara and Khulna ports and private jetties in the Khulna region.

Petroleum

Freight flows of petroleum products originate in Chattogram. Crude oil imported through Chattogram Port is refined at the Eastern Refinery of the Bangladesh Petroleum Corporation in Chattogram. Refined petroleum is also imported through Chattogram Port. Petroleum products are distributed from Chattogram to various depots across the country located close to river ports, where they are stored for further distribution. About 5 million tons a year of petroleum products are distributed to oil depots at Khulna, Dhaka, Narayanganj, Ashuganj, and Baghabari via inland waterways (map 2.12). They represent about 90 percent of all petroleum products distributed across the country; the remaining 10 percent is distributed by rail (8 percent) and roads (2 percent).

MAP 2.11

Freight flows of wheat on inland waterways in Bangladesh

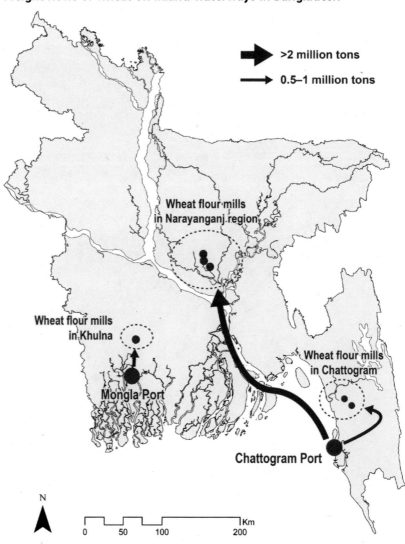

Source: PwC 2018.

Consumption of petroleum products is concentrated in the Dhaka and Chattogram region. Petroleum products are transported through inland waterways to intermediate depots at Godenail and Fatullah for distribution in the Dhaka region. These depots also help service demand for petroleum products in Bhairab, Ashuganj, and Chandpur. Petroleum products are transported through inland waterways to intermediate depots at Daulatpur and Baghabari to supply the northwest region. Distribution from Daulatpur depot to the northwest region then occurs through railways. Distribution of petroleum products in the northeast region is done by railway directly from Chattogram. The Barishal division is supplied by depots in Barishal and Jhalakathi, which receive petroleum products directly from Chattogram by waterway.

MAP 2.12

Freight flows of petroleum products in Bangladesh

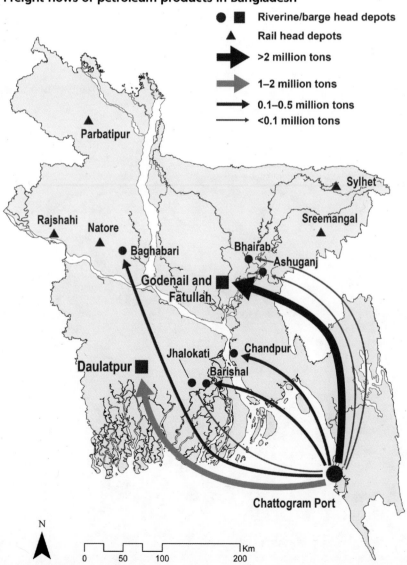

Source: PwC 2018.

Construction

About 17 million tons a year of construction material originate in the Sylhet region and are transported along the inland water transport network. These materials consist primarily of sand and stones. Multiple varieties of sand are used for construction in Bangladesh. The coarse sand originating at Sylhet is used to produce concrete. Meghna sand, which is extracted at multiple locations on the Meghna and Buriganga rivers, is also used in construction.[15] Stones originate in the Sylhet region, particularly in Chhatak, Sunamganj, and Jamalganj.

Construction materials are handled at various river ports and various construction sites of mega-infrastructure projects. The primary destination for construction materials is the Dhaka region, followed by the Khulna region (map 2.13). Typically, the area behind the port forms a construction

MAP 2.13

Freight flows of construction materials on inland waterways in Bangladesh

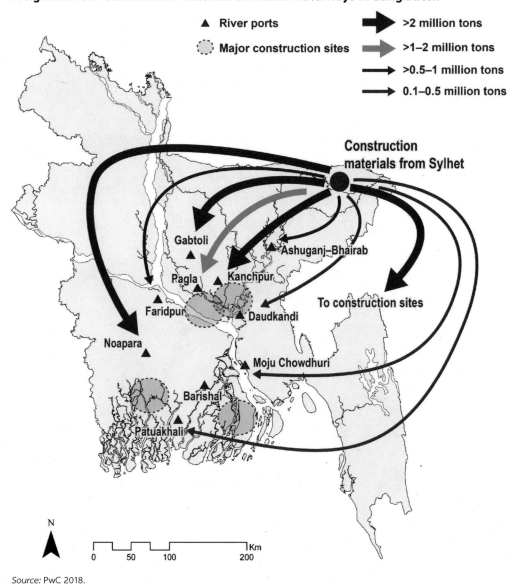

Source: PwC 2018.

market place. Pagla and Gabtoli are popular market places for construction materials.

FREIGHT MOVEMENT BY RAIL

Bangladesh has more than 450 railway stations, of which 55 handle almost all the freight carried by Bangladesh Railways. Between May 2016 and April 2017, just over 100,000 loaded freight wagons travelled between the 55 stations. The sections of the railway network with the heaviest traffic of freight wagons are the Dhaka–Chattogram corridor and the sections between the Rohanpur station (Nawabganj district) and the Sirajganj station (Sirajganj district) and between the Darshana station (Chuadanga district) and the Sirajganj station (Sirajganj district) (map 2.14).

MAP 2.14

Movements of freight wagons on railway network in Bangladesh, May 2016–April 2017

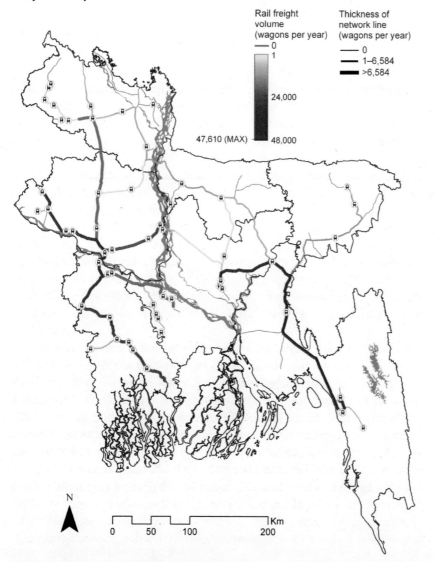

Source: World Bank, using data from Bangladesh Railways.

The Rohanpur and Darshana stations are on or close to the border with India; cargo originating there comes from India.

Between May 2016 and April 2017, Bangladesh Railways transported about 3.1 million tons of bulk cargo and 72,000 20-foot equivalent units (TEUs) of containerized freight between its main stations. Data collected from the main freight-generating railway stations provide a good picture of freight flows on the railways. The movement of containers takes place only between Dhaka and Chattogram, with a balanced flow in both directions (map 2.15). The bulk cargo transported by railways is largely stones and petroleum products, followed by dry oil cake, fly ash, fertilizer, and food grains (figure 2.10).

MAP 2.15

Container movements on railways in Bangladesh, May 2016–April 2017

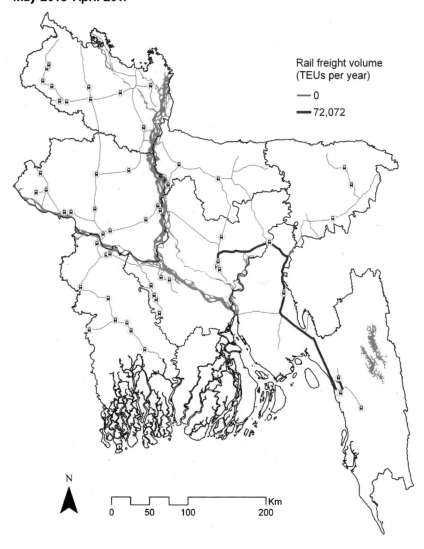

Rail freight volume
(TEUs per year)

— 0
— 72,072

N

0   50   100   200   Km

Source: World Bank, using data from Bangladesh Railways.

FIGURE 2.10
Bulk cargo on railways in Bangladesh, May 2016–April 2017

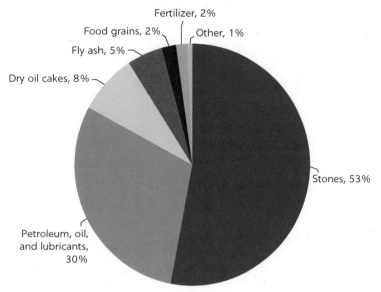

Source: World Bank, using data from Bangladesh Railways.

Bulk cargo movements on railways are clearly divided between the east and west sections of the network (map 2.16). The reason for the split is the limited connectivity between east and west sections. The Bangabandhu Bridge, the only bridge connecting east and west, has weight limitations because of the conditions of the bridge structure.

Petroleum products are the main bulk commodity transported by railways in the east. Forty percent of petroleum products on the railways are transported in the east, primarily along the south–north corridor from Chattogram to Sreemangal and Sylhet in the northeast. Very small volumes are transported in the opposite direction. Petroleum products originating in Chattogram are also unloaded in Cumilla, Dhaka, and Jamalpur. The second-most important bulk commodity transported in the east is fertilizer. About 32,000 tons a year of fertilizer (two-thirds of fertilizer moved on railways) originates at the Madgoan station, in Sylhet district. It is delivered to districts in the northwest.

The west section of the network carries the largest share of bulk cargo. All bulk commodities presented in figure 2.9 are transported in the west. The largest flows originate at the border with India, particularly at Rohanpur (1.1 million tons a year), Darshana (880,000 tons), and Benapole (87,000 tons). They go to Sirajganj and Faridpur, on the west banks of the Jamuna and Padma rivers. These commodities are transshipped to trucks and transported to destinations in the east of Bangladesh, indicating the importance of connecting east and west. The main commodities are stone chips (1.64 million tons a year), dry oil cakes (252,000 tons a year), and fly ash (153,000 tons a year). Another important commodity flow in the west is petroleum products, which originate in Khulna and are delivered to districts in the west, particularly the northwest.

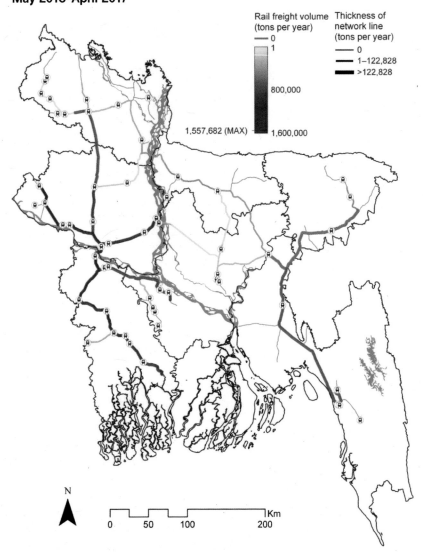

MAP 2.16

Bulk cargo movements on railways in Bangladesh, May 2016–April 2017

Rail freight volume (tons per year)

0

1

800,000

1,557,682 (MAX)

1,600,000

Thickness of network line (tons per year)

0

1–122,828

>122,828

N

| 0 | 50 | 100 | 200 | Km |

Source: World Bank, using data from Bangladesh Railways.

NOTES

1. Freight activity for construction; mining and quarrying; electricity; gas; steam and air conditioning supply; and water supply, sewerage, and waste management are either region specific or changeable over time. Because these sectors accounted for less than 1 percent of establishments and employment, they were not included in the survey. A significant number of establishments in Bangladesh are microenterprises, with one or two employees. Most of these enterprises sell their goods locally. As the intent of the analysis is to understand drivers and patterns of inter-district, not intra-city, freight flows, microenterprises were not considered.

2. Most people interviewed could provide information on freight generation in terms of boxes, pallets, numbers, or volumes rather than kilograms. Weights were estimated based on the standard weights of commodities and unit combinations. The significance of the freight generation models and the validity of the estimates are highly dependent on these estimates.

3. Freight generation was estimated for only 63 of the 64 districts in Bangladesh. Data from Kurigram district were missing from the census data.

4. The population from the Population and Housing Census 2011 was used to calculate freight generated per capita.

5. Freight generation of districts with (land, sea, and air) ports, such as Chattogram, is underestimated, because the estimates do not capture freight attraction of exports or freight production of imports, both of which take place outside the country.

6. Figure is based on traffic data collected by the Road and Highways Department at 934 stations across Bangladesh in 2013.

7. For consistency the freight attraction of imports and freight production of exports also needs to be removed from the freight generation estimates used in the FODS.

8. A medium truck equivalent has a payload of 20 tons.

9. Figure excludes exports through Chattogram port.

10. Figure excludes imports through Chattogram port.

11. Waterway depths are 3.5–4.0 meters for Class I, 2.1–3.5 meters for Class II, and 1.5–2.0 meters for Class III.

12. This figure is the number of vessels registered with the Department of Shipping under Inland Shipping Ordinance (1976) as of December 2016, according to BIWTA. Some vessels registered under the Merchant Shipping Ordinance (1983) also operate on inland waterways in Bangladesh. These are large vessels carrying dry and liquid bulk, mainly from Chattogram and Mongla ports to Dhaka and Narayanganj ports and between Chattogram and Mongla ports.

13. Movements of petroleum products are considered domestic because imported oil is refined and stored in the Chattogram area before the petroleum products are distributed across the country.

14. Factories in the Sylhet region import clinker and limestone from northeast India.

15. Because of the multiplicity of locations and the moving nature of these locations, flows of Meghna sand were not mapped.

REFERENCES

ADB (Asian Development Bank). 2012. *Capacity Building and Support to the Transport Sector Coordination Wing of the Planning Commission*. Final Report. Manila.

Andrés, L. A., D. Biller, and M. Herrera Dappe. 2013. *Reducing Poverty by Closing South Asia's Infrastructure Gap*. Washington, DC: World Bank.

BBS (Bangladesh Bureau of Statistics). 2010. *Agriculture Census 2008*. Government of Bangladesh, Ministry of Planning, Statistics and Informatics Division, Dhaka.

——. 2013. *Economic Census 2013*. Government of Bangladesh, Ministry of Planning, Statistics and Informatics Division, Dhaka.

Bird, J., Y. Li, H. Z. Rahman, M. Rama, and A. J. Venables. 2018. *Toward Great Dhaka: A New Urban Development Paradigm Eastward*. Directions in Development. Washington, DC: World Bank.

Holguín-Veras, J. 1984. *Definition of the Optimum Policy of Truck Import, 1984–1989*. Government of the Dominican Republic, Ministry of Public Works, Santo Domingo.

Holguín-Veras, J., and C. Gonzalez-Calderon. 2016. "Use of the Commodity Flow Survey Data to Estimate Freight Generation and Freight Trip Generation Models." In *Commodity Flow Survey Workshop*, 36–37. Washington, DC: Transportation Research Board, National Academies of Sciences, Engineering, and Medicine.

Holguín-Veras, J., S. Hodge, J. Wojtowicz, C. Singh, C. Wang, M. Jaller, F. Aros-Vera, K. Ozbay, M. Marsico, A. Weeks, M. Replogle, C. Ukegbu, J. Ban, M. Brom, S. Campbell, I. Sánchez-Díaz, C. González, A. Kornhauser, M. Simon, S. McSherry, A. Rahman, T. Encarnación, X. Yang, D. Ramirez-Rios, L. Kalahasthi, J. Amaya-Leal, M. Silas, B. Allen, and B. Cruz. 2018. "The New York City Off-Hour Deliveries Program: A Business and Community-Friendly Sustainability Program." *Interfaces* 48 (1): 70–86.

Holguín-Veras, J., M. Jaller, L. Destro, X. Ban, C. Lawson, and H.S. Levinson. 2011. "Freight Generation, Freight Trip Generation, and Perils of Using Constant

Trip Rates." *Transportation Research Record: Journal of the Transportation Research Board* 2224 (1): 68–81.

Holguín-Veras, J., C. Lawson, C. Wang, M. Jaller, C. González-Calderón, S. Campbell, L. Kalahashti, J. Wojtowicz, and D. Ramirez. 2016. *Using Commodity Flow Survey Microdata to Estimate the Generation of Freight, Freight Trip Generation, and Service Trips: Guidebook.* NCFRP Research Report 37, Transportation Research Board, Washington, DC. https://www.nap.edu/catalog/24602/using-commodity-flow-survey-microdata-and -other-establishment-data-to-estimate-the-generation-of-freight-freight-trips-and -service-trips-guidebook.

Holguín-Veras, J., and G. Patil. 2007. "Integrated Origin-Destination Synthesis Model for Freight with Commodity-Based and Empty Trip Models," *Transportation Research Record* 2008: 60–66.

——. 2008. "A Multi-commodity Integrated Freight Origin-Destination Synthesis Model." *Networks and Spatial Economics* 8(2–3): 309–26. http://dx.doi.org/10.1007/s11067-007 -9053-4.

Holguín-Veras, J., J. M. I. Sánchez-Díaz, S. Campbell, and C. Lawson. 2014. "Freight Generation and Freight Trip Generation Models." In *Modeling Freight Transport*, ed. L. Tavasszy and G. De Jong. Amsterdam: Elsevier.

Holguín-Veras, J., I. Sánchez-Díaz, C. T. Lawson, M. Jaller, S. Campbell, H.S. Levinson, and H. Shin. 2013. "Transferability of Freight Trip Generation Models." *Transport Research Record*, 2379: 1–8.

Holguín-Veras, J., and E. Thorson. 2003. "Practical Implications of Modeling Commercial Vehicle Empty Trips." *Transportation Research Record: Journal of the Transportation Research Board* 1833: 87–94.

Noortman, H.J., and J. Van Es. 1978. *Traffic Model. Manuscript for the Dutch Freight Transport Model.*

PwC. 2018. "Assessment of Freight Transportation and Logistics Market in Bangladesh." Background paper prepared for this report, World Bank, Washington, DC.

USDA (U.S. Department of Agriculture). 2017. Bangladesh Grain and Feed Update. Washington, DC. https://www.fas.usda.gov/data/bangladesh-grain-and-feed-update-9.

3 Logistics Costs

INTRODUCTION

The private costs of logistics refer to the costs incurred by a shipper. In addition to the price charged by the service provider or the cost of operating own assets (direct cost), the concept of generalized logistics costs considers the opportunity cost to the shipper of immobilized cargo during transport and storage and the cost associated with the level of service (indirect costs) (figure 3.1). Generalized logistics costs include all costs that are incurred by shippers to overcome the frictions of time and space (Tavasszy, Davydenko, and Ruijgrok 2009).

The social costs of logistics refer to the costs society incurs as a result of shippers' decision to ship their cargo. They are the sum of the private costs and the costs of logistics externalities. Logistics externalities include environmental emissions, crashes, noise, congestion and unrecovered costs associated with the provision, operation, and maintenance of public facilities.

This chapter presents estimates of the private logistics costs for key industries and the costs of externalities such as environmental emissions.

PRIVATE LOGISTICS COSTS

Methodology

Generalized logistics costs were estimated for nine industries (ready-made garments, leather footwear, pharmaceuticals, structural metal products, wooden furniture, jute products, rice milling, horticulture, and dairy), selected based on the following four criteria:

- Industry has economic relevance, based on value added, employment, and exports.
- Industry has potential to become economically relevant and is a priority in the Bangladesh Industrial Policy 2016.
- Industries have different logistics requirements.
- Industries provide broad geographical coverage.

Surveys and in-depth interviews were conducted with stakeholders on the demand and supply sides of the logistics service markets. A survey

FIGURE 3.1
Logistics costs

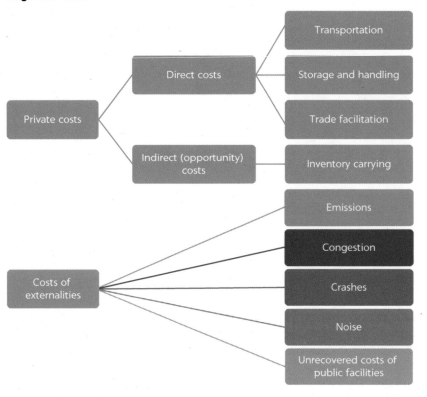

Source: World Bank analysis.

was administered to 400 economic establishments (shippers) with 10 or more employees.[1] The sample was stratified evenly among industries[2] and across districts based on the spatial distribution of establishments in each industry in the 2013 Economic Census. A survey of 253 logistics service providers across the spectrum of logistics services was also conducted. Its sample was stratified as follows: transport (road [100], inland water [25], air [6], sea [5], rail [2]); warehousing (50); freight forwarding (20); customs handling (20); less than container load (20); third-party logistics (5).

The surveys and in-depth interviews collected information that helped the study team understand and characterize the value chains in each industry. The surveys also collected detailed data on the costs and prices of logistics services. The generalized logistics costs for each industry were estimated using activity-based costing (appendix E presents a detailed discussion of the methodology used to calculate these costs). Private logistics costs estimates include only domestic costs (for example, the sea or air transport costs are not included for imported inputs or exported outputs).

Logistics costs estimates

Private logistics costs in Bangladesh are high in most sectors, ranging from 4.5 percent of sales for leather footwear to 47.9 percent of sales for horticulture (figure 3.2). Costs vary across sectors because of several factors. Industries with high-value products, such as leather footwear and ready-made garments, most of which are exported, have the lowest logistics costs as a percentage of sales.

FIGURE 3.2

Logistics costs in Bangladesh, by industry

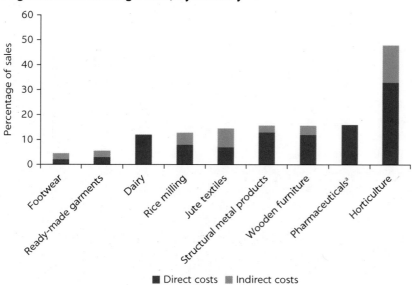

■ Direct costs ■ Indirect costs

Source: World Bank analysis.
a. Logistics costs for the pharmaceutical industry include only direct costs, as firms did not provide the information required to estimate inventory carrying costs.

FIGURE 3.3

Inventory carrying costs in Bangladesh, by industry

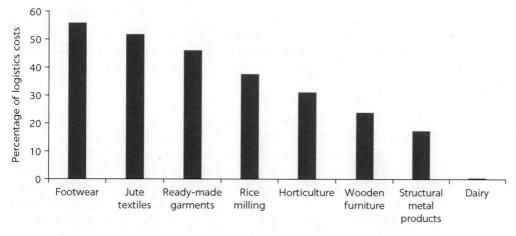

Source: World Bank analysis.

Low-value industries, such as horticulture, have the highest logistics costs as a percentage of sales. Industries that have complex logistics requirements, such as pharmaceuticals and dairy, have relatively high logistics costs.

Inventory carrying costs range from 0.05 percent of sales in the dairy industry to about 15 percent in the horticulture industry, with all other industries in the 2.5–7.5 percent range. Even in industries such as footwear and ready-made garments, where inventory carrying costs are low relative to sales, they represent a large share of private logistics costs (figure 3.3). In all industries except the dairy industry, inventory carrying costs represent 17–56 percent of private logistics costs, with the figure exceeding 30 percent in most industries.

To protect themselves against unreliability in the delivery of raw materials and finished products and congestion at gateways and along key corridors, firms in Bangladesh hold extra inventories. The share of firms that indicate inconsistencies in deliveries and congestion affect their inventory holdings is 75 percent in ready-made garments, 73 percent in wooden furniture, 68 percent in retail sale of groceries, 65 percent in structural metal, 55 percent in pharmaceutical products, and 53 percent in footwear. Export-oriented industries and industries relying on imported inputs, such as ready-made garments, footwear, and pharmaceuticals, maintain up to six months of inventories to mitigate the impact of unreliable deliveries and higher lead time caused by congestion at Chattogram Port. Higher inventory levels in industries such as rice milling, jute textiles, and horticulture are maintained largely because of the seasonality of raw materials.

Direct logistics costs range from 2 to 33 percent of sales, depending on the transport needs and the value of the final product (see figure 3.2). Transport costs represent the largest share of direct logistics costs in all sectors except ready-made garments, where it represents about a third of direct logistics costs. In industries that import inputs or export their outputs, trade facilitation costs represent a larger share of direct logistics costs than storage and handling costs. Transport costs as a share of direct logistics costs range from 31 to 100 percent (figure 3.4). As these industries rely exclusively on trucks to transport their inputs and outputs inside the country, transport costs represent the costs of hiring trucking services.

Transport costs and prices

Road transport rates in Bangladesh are high. Average trucking rates in per ton per kilometer range from $0.06 for a 16-ton truck to $0.12 for a trailer (figure 3.5). The most commonly used truck in Bangladesh is a seven-ton truck, the average

FIGURE 3.4

Components of direct logistics costs in Bangladesh, by industry

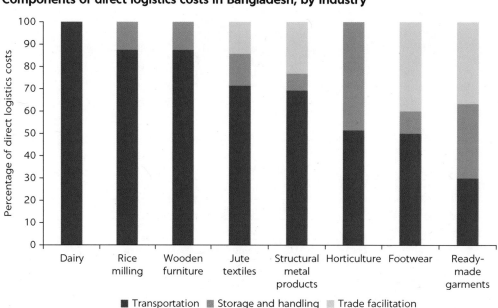

Source: World Bank analysis.
Note: Firms in the pharmaceutical industry did not provide the information required to estimate the components of direct logistics costs.

FIGURE 3.5

Trucking rates in selected countries

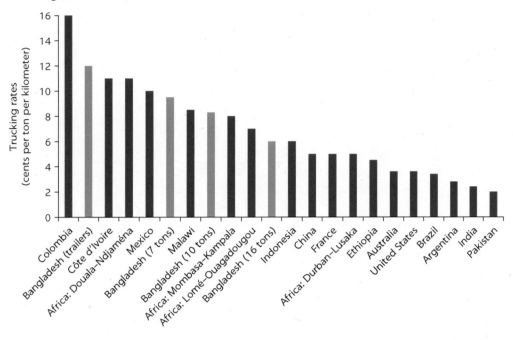

Source: Teravaninthorn and Raballand 2009, ADB 2016, and World Bank.

rate for which is $0.095 per ton per kilometer. These rates are higher than in many developing and developed countries (figure 3.5).

Several inefficiencies in the system explain the relatively high trucking rates. The costs of drivers and helpers; depreciation and interest; and fuel, insurance, registration, maintenance, and tires represent 71 percent of total trucking costs in Bangladesh (figure 3.6). Overhead and import duty costs represent another 4 percent of trucking costs. Accidents; facilitation payments to drivers unions, traffic police, ferry operators, and others; and broker fees represent the remaining 25 percent (box 3.1). On average a truck is involved in one major crash requiring significant repair and several minor crashes a year. The main reason for the crashes is unskilled drivers. Accident costs include repair costs, negotiated compensation to people injured or the families of people killed, and facilitation payments to police.

A comparison with the truck operating costs in Vietnam shows a similar breakdown once accident costs are excluded (Lam, Sriram, and Khera 2019). Facilitation payments, fuel cost, insurance, registration, taxes, and tolls cost 2 percentage points more in Bangladesh than in Vietnam. Repair, maintenance, and tires cost 5 percentage points more in Bangladesh than in Vietnam. Capital costs, administrative costs, and employment costs represent 4, 3, and 2 percentage points more in Vietnam than in Bangladesh.

A comparison with the United States excluding accident and administrative costs shows that insurance, tolls, registration, licensing, and taxes represent three times as much in Bangladesh (21 percent) as in the United States (7 percent). Fuel cost represents 50 percent more in Bangladesh (34 percent) than in the United States (22 percent). Employment costs represent a much larger share in the United States (43 percent) than in Bangladesh (18 percent) (Hooper and Murray 2018).

FIGURE 3.6

Breakdown of operating costs for seven-ton truck in Bangladesh

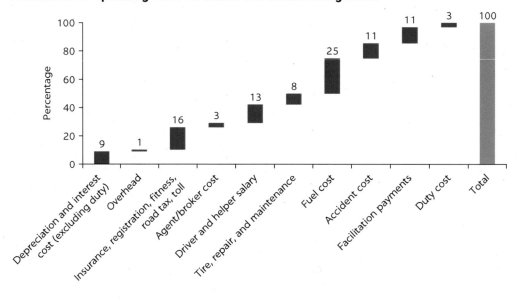

Source: World Bank analysis.

Facilitation payments in Bangladesh's transport sector

Shippers and carriers in Bangladesh regularly make payments—at ports, ferry crossings, border posts, and weighbridge stations—to expedite the movement of their goods and vehicles and to get a cargo allocation. Corrupt practices have long affected operations at Chattogram Port (Mahmud and Rossette 2007). Long delays getting cargo allocated to inland water transport are common unless informal payments are made, which results in low utilization of vessels. Without making payments at ferry crossings, it takes trucks 5–24 hours to cross rivers, which results in low utilization rates for trucks (number of days the vehicle is utilized out of the available days) and damage to perishable cargo. Truck owners also feel compelled to make facilitation payments to traffic police and labor unions to ensure smooth passage through different districts.

The involvement of associations has resulted in the creation of a market for intermediaries or agents. Industry players consulted for this study report that they have long-term arrangements with local agents who make facilitation payments on their behalf. Such payments are particularly common in industries that

ship time-sensitive and high-value goods. Payments are both to public sector officials and to associations. The facilitation payment component of the overall cost of road transport is about Tk 3,000–5,000 per round trip depending on the number of districts crossed and ferries used. On average, a truck pays Tk 100 to the drivers union and Tk 700 to the traffic police of each district crossed, as well as Tk 1,000 at each ferry crossing.

TABLE 3.1.1 **Facilitation payments in Bangladesh, by route**

ROUTE	TOTAL PAYMENTS (TK/ROUND TRIP)
Dhaka–Chattogram	3,200
Dhaka–Sylhet	3,200
Dhaka–Khulna	5,200
Dhaka–Rangpur	3,200
Dhaka–Jashore	5,200
Dhaka–Rajshahi	3,200
Dhaka–Benapole	5,200
Dhaka–Akhaura	3,200

Source: World Bank analysis.

FIGURE 3.7
Round-trip transport rates for 7- and 10-ton trucks in Bangladesh, by corridor

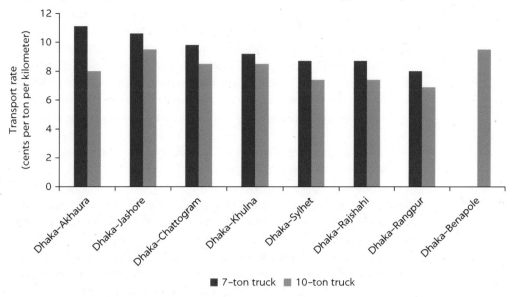

■ 7–ton truck ■ 10–ton truck

Source: World Bank analysis

Spatial differences in truck rates arise mainly from route-specific inefficiencies and operating practices. Figure 3.7 shows the rates charged by truck operators for the most common types of trucks (trucks with 7- and 10-ton carrying capacity) operating on various routes. The highest rate for 7-ton trucks is on the Dhaka–Akhaura route, which has shortest average distance (140 kilometers) among the routes compared. Rates are lowest on the Dhaka–Rangpur route, which has the longest one-way distance (about 310 kilometers). Facilitation payments on each route depend on the number of districts crossed and ferry crossing, as payments must be made to drivers unions and police in every district and to ferry operators (see box 3.1). The Dhaka–Chattogram route has a high per ton-kilometer tariff because transporters are not able to overload trucks travelling from Dhaka to Chattogram because of the low density of export cargo. Elsewhere drivers overload vehicles (overloading is discussed in chapter 4).

Low truck utilization increases average trucking costs, forcing truck operators to charge higher rates to be profitable. Field surveys indicate that the average utilization of a truck in Bangladesh is about 70 percent—lower than the 80 percent rate in Vietnam (Lam, Sriram, and Khera 2019). Inefficiencies at loading/unloading points, such as Chattogram Port, lead to long idle times for trucks. The very high levels of congestion across the country reduce travel speeds and increase travel times. These two inefficiencies, coupled with short shipping distances in Bangladesh (about 250–300 kilometers), lead to low truck utilization. The large share of empty truck trips, conservatively estimated at 35 percent, also contributes to low truck utilization. Trucking companies charge higher rates on routes that will require an empty return trip and that are more congested.

Limited competition for logistics services allows service providers to charge rates above marginal costs. Drivers unions and owners associations hold tight control over trucking rates and the allocation of cargo to service providers. In inland water transport, the Water Transport Cell, a legally constituted barge owners association, allocates imported cargo on a first come first served basis at fixed tariffs out of Chattogram Port. (Chapter 5 examines the role of unions and associations in setting tariffs and restricting competition.)

Trucking faces limited competition from rail and inland water transport, reinforcing trucking service providers' ability to charge rates above marginal costs. For example, the total cost of rail haulage between Chattogram and Dhaka and handling at the Kamalapur inland container depot is about $0.045 per ton-kilometers, which is lower than the truck tariff charged on the route. However, there is an additional cost for the last-mile transport in Dhaka, where two covered vans are used to carry the cargo from the depot to the consignee premises, at a cost of about $0.22 per ton-kilometer. Rail service is also very unreliable; the movement of cargo take several days, resulting in very low preference for rail among users. The transit time for railways on the Chattogram–Dhaka route is about 10–12 hours. Including the first-mile and last-mile travel time and the time taken for customs clearance at the Kamalapur depot, it takes two to three days to deliver cargo to its destination, far more than the single day by truck.

No significant inefficiencies affect the operation of inland water barges. Inefficiencies are in the cargo handling at ports and in first-/last-mile connectivity. Because of poor port infrastructure and manual handling, the number of monthly barge trips is low, resulting in low revenues. Where terminal handling is mechanized, the number of trips increases. Fuel and crew wages contribute 55 percent to the cost of barge operation, followed by depreciation and interest cost, overhead, and repair and maintenance cost (figure 3.8).

The cost of transporting a 20-foot equivalent unit (TEU) by inland waterway from Chattogram Port to the Pangaon container terminal in Dhaka is about $0.06 per ton-kilometer. Although the rate is half the $0.12 charged for a container trailer operating on the route, the cost advantage is eroded by the high last-mile cost to reach the consignee's premises. Because inland water transport is not extensively used for container movements, trucks operating between factories and Pangaon have to make an empty trip from the factory back to the terminal,

FIGURE 3.8

Breakdown of operating costs for a 1,000-ton barge in Bangladesh

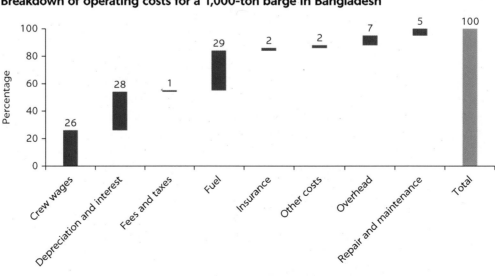

Source: World Bank analysis.

which increases the cost of road transport. Moreover, because the distance is short, truck rates are high, at about $0.22 per ton-kilometer.

The movement of containers through inland waterways takes several days, further hampering the competitiveness of inland water transport along the Dhaka–Chattogram corridor. Voyage times between Chattogram and Pangaon are 15–20 hours (depending on tidal variations). Loading and unloading the barges take another 10–12 hours. According to field surveys, cargo clearance at the Pangaon terminal takes about two to three days. As a result, the average door-to-door movement time is about five days, compared with less than a day by truck.

IMPACT OF CONGESTION ON LOGISTICS COSTS

Congestion in Bangladesh is a serious problem, not only in urban areas but also along inter-city roads. Speed data collected from more than 200 inter-city road segments (including national, regional, and district roads) across 26 districts shows an average speed of 30 kilometers an hour. Some of the reasons for congestion are the insufficient capacity of roads and bridges to handle current demand, the need to rely on inefficient ferries to cross rivers (because of the small number of bridges), the mismanaged system of weight checks at bridges; and policies, regulations, and procedures that create unnecessary trips. (Chapter 4 discusses these issues in detail.)

Congestion affects both direct and indirect logistics costs. It has a direct impact on fuel consumption and fleet requirements, as idling vehicles and stop-and-go traffic increase costs. Longer travel times also increase labor costs, because more hours are needed to complete deliveries. As congestion increases, so does the variability of travel times, which affects the reliability of shipments and hence shippers' inventory decisions and costs. Increased travel times also increases the opportunity costs of in-transit inventories.

The focus in this section is on the impact of congestion on inter-city road transport costs. To assess it, the study team installed GPS loggers on trucks transporting cargo along key inter-city corridors. The devices collected data on location, distances travelled, travel times, and speeds of trucks for two to four weeks, producing 79 usable observations (trips) along key inter-city corridors. Speeds, distance, and the duration of trips in uncongested conditions were estimated using Google Maps API and selecting off-hours to simulate travel under free-flow conditions.[3] Because the Google Maps data vary widely and are not as precise in Bangladesh as in other markets, the values obtained for distance traveled and travel times via this method provide higher values than those expected from "true" free-flow estimates.

The GPS data collected confirm that congestion is a serious problem in Bangladesh. The average trip length in the sample in actual conditions is 114 kilometers, almost the same as in uncongested conditions, because of the limited options in Bangladesh's road network (table 3.1). The average duration of a trip in actual conditions is 18 hours—more than 6 times the 2.8 hours in uncongested conditions. The average speed in actual conditions is 19 kilometers an hour—less than half the average speed in uncongested conditions of 40 kilometers an hour.

Congestion is prevalent across the country. The 79 routes were grouped into seven corridors or regions: Dhaka–Chattogram, Dhaka–northwest, Dhaka–Mymensigh, Dhaka–northeast, Dhaka–southwest, east corridor, and Greater Dhaka.[4] Figure 3.9 shows that congestion is prevalent in all corridors and regions

TABLE 3.1 **Summary statistics for actual and uncongested conditions for sampled truck trips**

VARIABLE	MEAN		MINIMUM		MAXIMUM	
	UNCONGESTED	ACTUAL	UNCONGESTED	ACTUAL	UNCONGESTED	ACTUAL
Distance (kilometers)	113	114	20	20	318	306
Duration (hours)	2.8	18.0	0.7	2.5	7.4	96.2
Speed (kilometers/hour)	40	19	20	0.4	60	36

Source: World Bank analysis.

FIGURE 3.9

Actual versus free-flow travel time in Bangladesh, by corridor

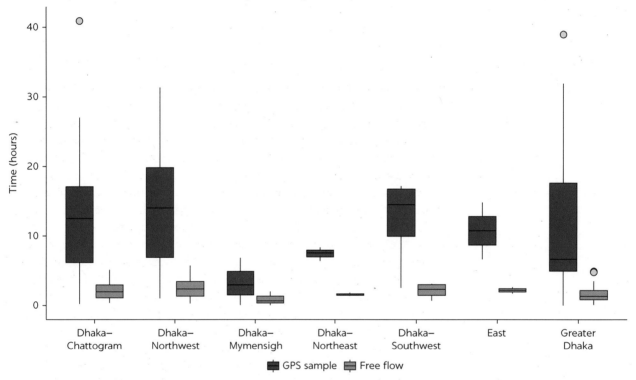

Source: World Bank analysis.
Note: The bottom of a box represents the first quartile, the middle bar the second quartile (median), and the top of the box the third quartile. The whiskers represent the highest and lowest values, excluding outliers. The dots are outliers.

covered, with median travel time in actual conditions (GPS sample) much higher than in uncongested conditions (free flow).

Comparing the costs of traveling with and without congestion shows the impact of congestion on transport costs. The Travel Congestion Index (TCI), defined as the percentage increase in transport costs over uncongested conditions, captures the impact of congestion on transport costs (Holguín-Veras, Encarnación, González-Calderón, Cantillo and others 2016). Standard trucking unit costs per hour (the labor costs of the driver and helper, depreciation, and interest) and per kilometer (the cost of fuel, insurance, registration, maintenance, and tires) were used to estimate transport costs in congested and uncongested conditions. The TCI for a trip is defined as follows:

$$TCI = \left(\frac{transport\ cost\ in\ congested\ conditions}{transport\ cost\ in\ uncongested\ conditions} - 1 \right) \times 100\% \qquad (3.1)$$

TABLE 3.2 Travel Congestion Index in Bangladesh, by corridor

CORRIDOR/REGION	NUMBER OF OBSERVATIONS	TRAVEL CONGESTION INDEX (PERCENT)		
		MEAN	MINIMUM	MAXIMUM
Dhaka–Chattogram	41	120	7	410
Dhaka–northwest	18	79	7	365
Dhaka–southwest	4	129	57	199
Dhaka–northeast	3	8	6	11
Dhaka–Mymensingh	1	6	6	6
East	2	11	7	16
Greater Dhaka	33	125	7	1,072

Source: World Bank analysis.

Congestion has a huge impact on direct logistics costs in Bangladesh, doubling average standard trucking costs.[5] Standard trucking costs represent 71 percent of total trucking costs. If there were no congestion in Bangladesh, total costs borne by truck operators would therefore be 35.5 percent lower on average. If trucks operators passed the reductions in costs on to shippers—which is unlikely, given the limited competition in the sector—direct logistics costs for the eight industries studied (footwear, ready-made garment, dairy, horticulture, jute products, rice milling, wooden furniture, and structural metal products) would be 11–36 percent lower.

Reductions in congestion would also reduce inventory carrying costs. The average in-transit inventory carrying cost would decrease by 84 percent (table 3.2). The in-transit component of inventory carrying costs is small compared with the in-storage component, as firms hold inventories for long periods in Bangladesh. Therefore, the potential reduction in inventory carrying costs would be small, unless firms shrank their inventories in response to reductions in congestion, which would also decrease the cost of storage.

The impact of congestion on inter-city road transport along the northwest-southeast axis is significant. The corridors along the northwest-southeast axis are the backbone of Bangladesh, facing the highest demand from freight transport (see chapter 2). Congestion increases average standard trucking costs in Greater Dhaka by 125 percent, along the Dhaka–Chattogram corridor by 120 percent, and along the Dhaka–northwest corridor by 79 percent (see table 3.2). Congestion along the Dhaka–southwest corridor increases trucking operating costs by 129 percent. This result and the results for the Dhaka–northeast, Dhaka–Mymensingh, and east corridors should be interpreted with care, however, as the number of observations is very small (one to four).

COSTS OF LOGISTICS EXTERNALITIES

Externalities of logistics operations include environmental emissions, crashes, congestion, noise, and unrecovered costs associated with the provision, operation, and maintenance of public facilities. Logistics operations, particularly fossil fueled freight vehicles, emit pollutants and noises that are harmful to the environment and human health. Freight vehicles cause crashes. Overloaded trucks damage roads. Freight vehicles take road space from other vehicles, adding to congestion.

Estimating the costs of each these externalities is challenging, as the data requirements are significant. This section discusses evidence on the importance of the externalities of truck overloading and accidents and presents estimates of the costs of emissions and the impact of congestion on the latter.

Overloading of trucks

The overloading of trucks is a major contributor to the deterioration of roads. Truck operators report that they load more than 50 percent over the allowed limit, in order to improve their profitability. They do so by modifying their vehicles and bypassing the process to obtain and renew annual fitness certificates by making facilitation payments.

Operators indicate that overloading of medium trucks, the most common truck size in Bangladesh, is in the 70–80 percent range. The damage to the roads caused by a medium truck with this level of overloading is about four times the damage caused by a truck with no overloading.[6]

Vehicle crashes

The number of road injuries and fatalities in Bangladesh is high, with trucks playing an important role. According to the Global Burden of Disease (2016), road crashes in Bangladesh resulted in 1.15 million disability-adjusted life years (DALYs) in 2016.[7] Results of the survey of transporters reveal that on average a truck is involved in one major crash and several minor crashes a year. The consequences of minor crashes are minor damage to trucks and no injuries; the consequences of major crashes are heavy damage to vehicles, injuries, and even fatalities.

The main reason for the large number of crashes involving trucks is unskilled drivers. Without detail information on the share of DALYs caused by truck-related crashes, quantification of the social cost of crashes attributed to the logistics sector is not feasible. However, the evidence suggests it is not negligible.

Emissions

A computer program developed by Holguín-Veras, Encarnación, González-Calderón, Winebrake and others (2016) was used to estimate emissions of seven pollutants: carbon dioxide (CO_2), carbon monoxide, nitrogen oxides, total organic gases, reactive organic gases, and particulate matter with aerodynamic diameters of less than 10 μm (PM_{10}) and 2.5 μm ($PM_{2.5}$). The program reads the GPS data and applies the appropriate emission factors corresponding to truck type, model year, fuel type, and speed over the course of the travelled route. Emission rates per kilometer were multiplied by the number of kilometers travelled by trucks estimated by the freight origin-destination synthesis (FODS) to obtain total emissions from inter-district trucking in Bangladesh.

The estimates provided should serve as a lower bound of the environmental emissions produced by truck traffic. The emission factors used in the software come from the EMFAC Web Database (California Environmental Protection Agency 2016). This software is designed for conditions in the United States. However, by considering the type of truck, year, fuel type, and distance, the results can replicate emissions produced in Bangladesh with some degree of confidence, except for effects corresponding to meteorology, which the models

TABLE 3.3 **Environmental emissions from inter-city road freight transport in Bangladesh**

TYPE OF EMISSION	ANNUAL EMISSIONS (TONS)	PERCENT ATTRIBUTABLE TO CONGESTION
Reactive organic gases	69	73
Total organic gases	69	73
PM_{10}	21	70
$PM_{2.5}$	20	70
Nitrogen oxides	771	66
Carbon dioxide	90,127,436	55
Carbon monoxide	1,114,407	50

Source: World Bank analysis.
Note: PM_{10} and $PM_{2.5}$ refer to particulate matter with aerodynamic diameters of less than 10 and 2.5 μm, respectively.

cannot capture. The fabrication year of trucks in the sample ranges from 2013 to 2017. The average truck operating in Bangladesh is older than the average truck in the sample, and older trucks pollute more than newer trucks. Hence actual pollution is expected to be higher than the estimates presented in this section.

The social value of annual CO_2 emissions from inter-district road freight transport is $3 billion, or 1.2 percent of Bangladesh's GDP. Table 3.3 shows the environmental emissions of the seven pollutants considered. The estimation of the social value of annual CO_2 emissions is based on a social value of carbon of $33.17 (in 2017 dollars), which multiplied by the 90.1 million tons of CO_2 emitted annually by trucks yields a social value of $3 billion.[8]

The impact of congestion on emissions from inter-district road freight transport is substantial. About 50–73 percent of emissions of pollutants from trucks on inter-district trips are from congestion (see table 3.3). If there were no congestion in Bangladesh, CO_2 emissions would fall by more than half. The social value of such a reduction would be $1.63 billion a year (in 2017 dollars), or 0.7 percent of Bangladesh GDP.

NOTES

1. For companies with more than one establishment in which the logistics decisions are made centrally at headquarters, only one establishment was selected for the survey.
2. The establishment survey covered 10 industries, the 9 listed above plus retail sale of groceries. Logistics costs were not estimated for retail sale of groceries, because the industry is dominated by small retailers (open-air temporary shops, roadside shops, convenience stores). The transport of finished goods is carried out by manufacturers, with the logistic cost incorporated into the retail price. Small retail shops do not warehouse to maintain sufficient inventories.
3. There are several methods for estimating uncongested (free-flow) travel conditions. They require complete network data, including a fully connected network at street level, and attributes of the roads, including maximum speeds. Some of these data are not available for Bangladesh's road network.
4. When routes traverse more than one corridor or region, only the segment on the corridor or in the region was allocated to the corresponding group.
5. The travel congestion index ranges from 6-566 percent in the sample, with a standard deviation of 107 percent.
6. This estimation is based on the widely used rule-of-thumb that assumes that the damage of an axle-load is a function of the fourth power of the ratio between the actual axle-load

and the designed axle-load. A typical medium truck in Bangladesh has a maximum gross vehicle weight (including the cargo and the truck) of 16 tons. Overloading by 70–80 percent more cargo becomes 22 tons. The estimation can be seen as a lower bound for Bangladesh, as it assumes stronger pavements than those in the country.

7. Disability-adjusted life years is defined as the sum of years of potential life lost to premature mortality and years of productive life lost to disability.

8. The World Bank Group guidance note on the social value of carbon (SVC) proposes an SVC of $30 (in 2014 dollars) for 2015 and $35 for 2020 in its base case. The SVC was extrapolated to arrive at a value of $32 for 2017 and converted to 2017 dollars to yield a value of $33.17.

REFERENCES

ADB (Asian Development Bank). 2016. *Myanmar Transport Sector Policy Note: How to Reduce Transport Costs.* Mandaluyong City, Philippines.

California Environmental Protection Agency. 2016. EMFAC Web Database. https://www.arb.ca.gov/emfac/.

Global Burden of Disease. 2016. https://vizhub.healthdata.org/gbd-compare/.

Holguín-Veras, J., T. Encarnación, C. Gonzalez- Calderón, V. Cantillo, H. Yoshizaki, R. Garrido, L. Kalahasthi, and S. Kyle. 2016. *Methodology to Analyze and Quantify the Impacts of Congestion on Supply Chains in Latin-American Cities.* Inter-American Development Bank, Infrastructure and Environment Sector, Transportation Division, Washington, DC.

Holguín-Veras, J., T. Encarnación, C. A. González-Calderón, J. Winebrake, C. Wang, S. Kyle, N. Herazo-Padilla, L. Kalahasthi, W. Adarme, V. Cantillo, H. Yoshizaki, and R. Garrido. 2016. "Direct Impacts of Off-Hour Deliveries on Urban Freight Emissions." *Transportation Research Part D: Transport and Environment*: 1–20.

Hooper, A., and D. Murray. 2018. *An Analysis of Operational Costs of Trucking: 2018 Update.* American Transportation Research Institute. Arlington, Virginia.

Lam, Y.Y., K. Sriram, and N. Khera. 2019. *Strengthening Vietnam's Trucking Sector: Towards Lower Logistics Costs and Greenhouse Gas Emissions.* Directions in Development. Washington, DC: World Bank.

Mahmud, T., and J. Rossette. 2007. *Problems and Potentials of Chattogram Port: A Follow-Up Diagnostic Study.* www.ti-bangladesh.org /research /ES_CTG_ Port2007%28eng%29.pdf.

Tavasszy, L., I. Davydenko, and K. Ruijgrok. 2009. *The Extended Generalized Cost Concept and Its Application in Freight Transport and General Equilibrium Modeling.* http://resolver.tudelft.nl/uuid:153ec148-efa4-4a16-bfbf-c129a7dd3d6b.

Teravaninthorn, S., and G. Raballand. 2009. *Transport Prices and Costs in Africa: A Review of the Main International Corridors.* Directions in Development. Washington, DC: World Bank.

4 Logistics Infrastructure

INTRODUCTION

Good-quality and efficiently managed logistics infrastructure forms the backbone of any modern multimodal logistics system. Weaknesses in its logistics infrastructure have long been a challenge to realizing Bangladesh's potential for multimodal logistics and sustaining a high rate of economic growth. In 2018 Bangladesh ranked 99th among 140 economies in terms of its transport infrastructure in the World Economic Forum's Global Competitiveness Index; it ranked 127th among 205 economies in terms of quality of its trade and transport infrastructure on the World Bank's Logistics Performance Index.

This chapter discusses the core infrastructure challenges affecting logistics costs and explores the main issues affecting governance of transport and logistics infrastructure, public funding of infrastructure, private sector participation in infrastructure, and policies and regulations.

CHALLENGES

Inadequate capacity and inefficient operation

Bangladesh has invested considerable resources in infrastructure, but the transport and logistics system has not been able to keep up with the country's high rate of economic growth. Inefficient operation of infrastructure has also reduced the capacity of existing infrastructure. As a result, capacity constraints exist across the entire system.

Seaports

The core nodes of the transport system are the two main trade gateways of Chattogram and Mongla. Chattogram Port handles about 90 percent of sea-going cargo in Bangladesh, with the remaining cargo handled by Mongla Port. For containers the split is even more uneven, with Chattogram handling more than 98 percent of containers. Mongla's role is limited because it faces challenges with respect to draft availability, handling infrastructure, and connectivity to industrial clusters and consumption centers.

Chattogram is the deepest port in Bangladesh, but at 9.1 meters it is much shallower than other South Asian ports. As a result, Bangladesh's exports have to be carried in feeder vessels to the region's hub ports of Colombo, Singapore, and Tanjung Pelepas to link up with deep-sea services. The port suffers from severe capacity constraints associated with inadequate infrastructure and processes. Because of limited storage capacity and inefficient yard operation, empty containers (generated by the trade imbalance) are transported to the off-docks. They must be transported back to the port from the off-docks for export, adding to congestion within the city. Because of the limited number of cranes to handle containers, the port relies on less efficient vessel-mounted cranes to handle large numbers of containers. Because of vehicle congestion inside the port, the absence of separate weighbridges for the entry and exit movement of vehicles, and the slow uplift of containers in the storage yard, the few port cranes at the port work at only 8–12 cycles an hour instead of the optimal 22–28. These inefficiencies led to an average pre-berthing waiting time at Chattogram of 10 days, which was also highly variable as a result of frequent crane breakdowns. The commissioning of six new cranes will help reduce average waiting time and variability, but it will not be enough to remove the severe capacity constraints.

Inland transport: Roads, railways, and waterways

Bangladesh's high rate of growth is straining the road network. Traffic volumes above design capacity have resulted in congestion. The average speed on intercity roads in most districts is no more than 30 kilometers an hour, significantly raising logistics costs (as discussed in chapter 3).

Most investment has targeted the road sector; only limited improvements have been made to boost the use of other modes of transport, especially rail and river. Rail infrastructure (tracks and bridges) has not been upgraded to reflect current requirements, limiting the load-carrying capacity. The mostly single-track railway and the shortage of properly functioning rolling stock (locomotives and wagons) cause delays, especially in the Dhaka–Chattogram corridor.[1] The single track acts as a major bottleneck, limiting the number of trains that can run on the route.

Bangladesh's extensive river network (map 4.1) presents challenges for its navigation. The larger rivers are up to 50 meters deep, and most of the lower Meghna River (the main route on the Dhaka-Chattogram Corridor) is 10–25 meters deep. Bars have very shallow depths, however, especially at the confluences of the major rivers and their tributaries, at river bends, and in the wide delta area, limiting navigation. Poor navigation aid systems and very limited night-time aids also limit safe navigation.

The lack of bridges in strategic locations hinders the flow of road traffic. The vast network of rivers requires river crossings for almost all long-haul routes. Some critical locations have no bridges, especially connecting the southwest to eastern regions, at least until the Padma Bridge is completed. Ferry services are notoriously unreliable, as they are often disrupted by weather conditions and the breakdown of vessels. Waiting lines for ferries are usually long. Facilitation payments are often made to local agents to fast-track the ferry-crossing process, which increases logistics costs (see chapter 3). Where bridges are available, they often act as traffic bottlenecks, because they are either narrower than the approach highways or lack well-managed systems of weight controls.

The railway network also suffers from interconnectivity problems, caused by the dense river network and differences in gauges. It has two divisions, one in the east and the other in the west, separated by the Jamuna River (map 4.2). Most of

MAP 4.1
Bangladesh's river network

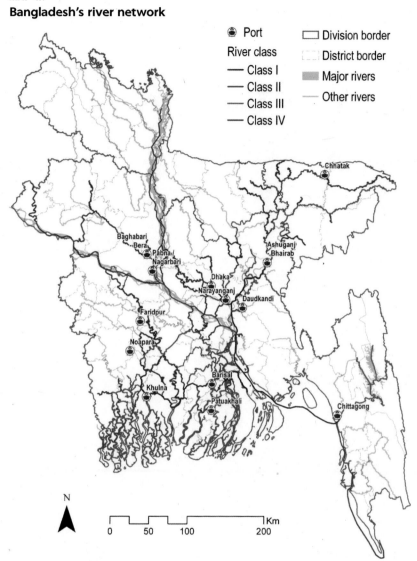

Source: World Bank, using data from HaskoningDHV 2016.
Note: Depth is 3.66-3.96 meters in Class I, 2.10-2.44 meters in Class II, 1.52-1.83 meters in Class III, and less than 1.52 meters in Class IV.

the tracks in the east are meter gauge, whereas in the west there are meter and broad-gauge tracks. The Bangabandhu Bridge, which opened in 1998, includes a railway connection, but it has structural problems that limit the loads that can be transported by rail. The Padma Bridge, which is under construction, and planned bridges such as the Jamuna dedicated rail bridge and the second Padma Bridge, will provide additional railway connections between east and west Bangladesh.

Air transport

The share of cargo transported by air is limited, but it has increased in recent years. Combining domestic and international cargo, volume amounted to about 260,000 tons in 2015. Ninety percent is handled by the country's main international airport, the Hazrat Shahjalal International Airport. Space restrictions at the airport and a ban by the European Union on cargo from Bangladesh imposed because of safety concerns has considerably hampered traffic (JICA 2017).

MAP 4.2
Bangladesh's railway network

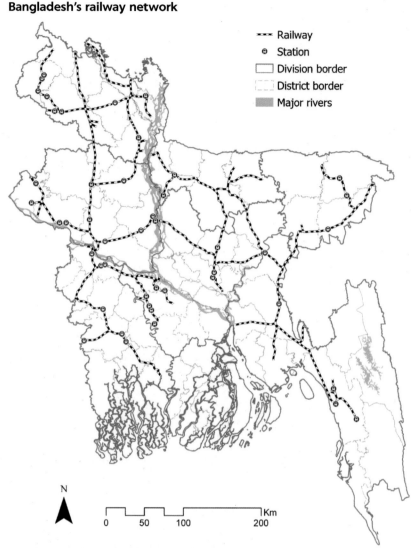

Legend:
- - - - Railway
- ⊙ Station
- ☐ Division border
- ☐ District border
- ▬ Major rivers

Source: World Bank, using data from Bangladesh Railways.

Biman Bangladesh, the government-owned airlines, is the only ground-handling agent at Shahjalal. It lacks skilled manpower and needed infrastructure, such as cargo-handling equipment, warehouse space, facilities for handling perishable and temperature-sensitive cargo, and appropriate scanning equipment. The warehouses at the airport are not sufficient to handle the volume of cargo. As a result, imported cargo is often left at the parking bays, exposing it to damage and theft. The X-ray scanners for scanning export cargo are not sufficient to handle the volume of cargo, which causes delays. The airport also lacks an explosive detection system (EDS) facility, which is required to get the necessary approval (RA-3) to ship goods directly to the European Union. Air cargo carriers consequently need to take the cargo to their hubs or Dubai airport for EDS scanning before exporting it to Europe. In view of the high cost, some major airlines have stopped operating freighters at Shahjalal.

Land ports

Bangladesh has 13 operational land ports. All of them suffer from poor infrastructure for handling, screening, and storing cargo and operational practices (Nyenrode Business Universitaet 2014). The customs clearance processes at land ports act as a bottleneck, as manual screening of cargo is performed at bonded warehouses after cargo is unloaded (vehicle-scanning machines are not available). At the Benapole land port, warehousing space is adequate for unloading cargo of about 3,000 trucks, but the dwell time of up to 10 days caused by delays in customs assessment reduces the effective capacity by a factor of 10. The lack of warehousing space and the absence of parking facilities forces trucks to line up on the access roads, increasing congestion in the surrounding areas.

Warehousing

The supply of proper warehouse structures is limited and concentrated in Dhaka and Chattogram, where most manufacturing, exports, and consumption takes place (Knight Frank 2017). Dhaka has evolved as a central warehousing hub for consumer goods aimed at the domestic and international markets. Chattogram serves as the main seaborne trade gateway and has consequently become the most important location for export-import warehousing. Dhaka and Chattogram account for approximately 70 percent of the warehousing space in Bangladesh (Knight Frank 2017). Other regional warehousing clusters or distribution hubs have emerged in various parts of Bangladesh, including Khulna, Sylhet, Barishal, Bogura, and Rangpur. The centers act as distribution hubs and cater to regional demand.

Limited intermodal integration

Most of Bangladesh's transport infrastructure was developed in "silos," which led to poor integration between modes. River ports are poorly connected to the road network and to economic centers. Access to river terminals in Dhaka is through a particularly narrow and congested road, for example. As a result, it takes a long time to reach the terminals, which leads to high trucking costs. At night, when traffic is not an issue, road security and theft along the route to the terminals discourage shippers from using river transport.

The evacuation and handling infrastructure, and the operational practices at river ports are suboptimal. Ports along the river routes lack adequate permanent berthing facilities; as a result, cargo is loaded and unloaded on temporary jetties. The lack of cargo-handling infrastructure at river ports leads to nonmechanized operations and high loading/unloading times, reducing the utilization of both barges and jetties and increasing operating costs. River ports also lack storage infrastructure. Cargo that is unloaded at the ports is often kept in the wharf area covered only by a tarpaulin, without security measures, exposing it to the risk of both theft and damage.

The limited capacity and operational inefficiencies at Chattogram Port hinder the access of river vessels loaded with containers. Although there is a dedicated berth for river vessels at Chattogram Port, it is used to handle import containers, because of severe congestion at Chattogram. The crane at the berth has been nonoperational for some years, further impeding the handling of barges without onboard cranes.

Kamalapur, in Dhaka, is the only functional rail-based inland container depot in Bangladesh; it is connected to Chattogram Port. The annual container-handling capacity of the depot is 90,000 TEUs. However, because of extremely long dwell times, its effective capacity has been reached, limiting growth in the corridor. Kamalapur is located inside Dhaka, in a congested area with narrow streets. Because of restrictions to movement of trucks in the city, trucks can access it only at night. Parking, both inside and near the terminal, is limited, increasing congestion (Gibson 2015).

Even when modes are physically interconnected, operational practices are often substantially different, making smooth integration difficult. For example, Chattogram Port and Bangladesh Railways collect different registration data from transporters, requiring the information to be collected twice, which delays shipments (Gibson 2015).

Limited regional integration

Bangladesh and India have basic interconnected road and rail networks, but differences in standards, market access policies, axle-load limits, and quality requirements hamper road and rail transport operations. For the same class of trucks, axle-load limits are lower in Bangladesh than in India (table 4.1). The differences could reflect weaker pavements in Bangladesh or a regulatory legacy in which limits have not kept pace with trends in trucking technology. The differences are cited as one reason for denying India transit rights across Bangladeshi territory. Railways in the region have a combination of meter and broad-gauge lines, limiting cross-border movements. Bangladesh has had to construct both gauges in some parts of the network to interface with the Indian system.

Accommodating differences in infrastructure is costly in terms of both time and money. Less costly to change are constraints imposed by different countries' policy choices. It is important that countries in the region harmonize their infrastructure standards to ensure the interoperability of transport systems. Doing so would enable vehicles and trains to travel across borders without the need for costly transloading.

Poor quality of transport infrastructure

The inadequate quality of transport infrastructure raises transport costs in Bangladesh. A condition survey conducted in 2017 classified more than 26 percent of the country's primary roads as being in poor, bad, or very bad condition, resulting in frequent breakdowns of vehicles, consequent congestion, and higher costs (Bangladesh Roads and Highways Department 2018). Industry players and logistics service providers cite poor road conditions in Bangladesh as a major

TABLE 4.1 **Gross vehicle weight limits in Bangladesh and India, by number of axles (tons)**

NUMBER OF AXLES	BANGLADESH	INDIA
3 (1 front, 2 back)	22	25
4 (steering + 3 axles)	25	31
5 (3 prime mover, 2 trailer)	38	44
6 (3 prime mover, 3 trailer)	41	44
7 (3 prime mover, 4 axles)	44	—

Source: World Bank estimates.
Note: — = not available.

factor behind long travel times and high costs (figure 4.1). Although there has been a significant improvement in road condition on the Dhaka–Chattogram route and within Dhaka city, roads along other key routes, such as Dhaka–Sylhet, Dhaka–Benapole and Dhaka–Rangpur, are broken and unmaintained.

Bangladesh lacks adequate monitoring and load enforcement infrastructure to ensure that trucks are not overloaded. As a result, transport operators often overload their trucks by more than 50 percent. Only a few road sections, such as those leading to the major bridges, have weight scales—and even on these routes, transporters circumvent the rules by offloading excess cargo to another truck just before the weight scale and reloading the cargo after crossing the bridge. When they are caught, carriers simply pay facilitation payments to traffic police and other monitoring authorities to avoid penalties. Carriers also make facilitation payments to the Bangladesh Road Transport Authority to obtain fitness certificates for modified trucks that allow them to overload.

Lack of maintenance constrains the accessibility of both inland waterways and railways. Because of lack of dredging and regular maintenance, only 25 percent of inland waterways are accessible in the monsoon season—and the figure drops to 16 percent during the dry season. Usage of inland waterways as a means of transport is therefore not a viable option along some routes. For example, because of the shallowness of sections of the river in the Rajshahi and Rangpur regions, rice producers cannot use inland waterways for transport, as the nearest inland water terminals (Baghabari and Nagarbari) are at least 200 kilometers away. Limited maintenance and rehabilitation of rail tracks and bridges limits the load-carrying capacity and potential speed of railways in Bangladesh.

Exposure to extreme weather events

Bangladesh's exposure to natural disasters represents an important challenge for transport infrastructure. Large sections of Bangladesh's transport network are exposed to natural disasters and at risk of disruptions (map 4.3). More than half of all road types are exposed to flooding, according to multihazard risk assessments by the Bangladesh Ministry of Disaster and Relief. The impacts of

FIGURE 4.1

Reasons for delays in shipments in Bangladesh, according to users

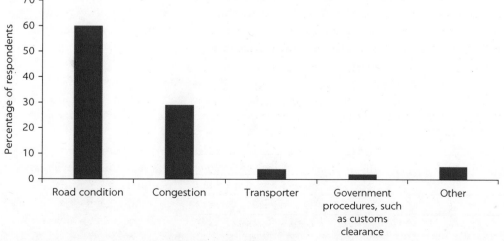

Source: Survey of logistics service providers conducted for this study.

MAP 4.3

Flood exposure of Bangladesh's road and inland waterway networks

a. Road network   b. Inland waterway network

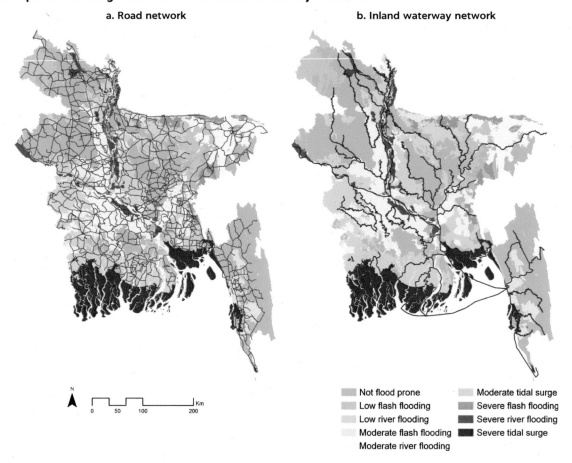

Not flood prone
Low flash flooding
Low river flooding
Moderate flash flooding
Moderate river flooding

Moderate tidal surge
Severe flash flooding
Severe river flooding
Severe tidal surge

Source: TU Delft 2018.

natural disasters on transport infrastructure have already been significant. Cyclone Sidr, in 2007, washed away a large number of roads and destroyed and damaged about 80 percent of equipment at ports and landing stations in the Khulna and Barishal Divisions (BanDUDeltAS 2015). Climate change will exacerbate these risks.

Climate-proofing transport infrastructure is costly. It is therefore important to concentrate investments where they will have the greatest impact, by identifying the infrastructure assets that would lead to the highest costs for sectors of the economy or communities if they failed.

Using the origin-destination matrix presented in chapter 2, TU Delft (2018) identified the most critical transport infrastructure in Bangladesh. Results from the analysis could be used to prioritize maintenance budget and transport infrastructure investments.

The critical inland segments are along the northwest-southeast corridor (TU Delft 2018), the backbone of the country. The Feni–Chattogram section of the N1 highway connecting Dhaka and Chattogram is the most critical segment, because it is the only land connection between the capital city of Dhaka and Chattogram Port. The Mirzapur–Joydebpur N4 corridor, which connects Dhaka with the western districts, is another critical segment. Along this corridor the Bangabandhu Bridge on N405—the only bridge crossing the Jamuna River—is particularly critical. Disruptions of the bridge would impose significant costs on the entire country, particularly the western districts. The N5 national highway in Bogura, which connects the Bangabandhu Bridge with northwest districts, and the waterway route between the Chattogram Port and Meghna River estuary are also critical.

Chattogram Port, the most vital and busiest port in Bangladesh, has almost no redundancy. Improving the Mongla Port could potentially be a good strategy for increasing the resilience of the economy during floods. When there is no flooding, the inland ports and *ghats* along the Meghna and Padma rivers are the most critical. Although less busy, inland ports and *ghats* in Khulna division, Barishal division, and the southern part of Dhaka division are critical for smaller transport activities. Improving waterways in these divisions would increase the resilience of the whole transport system.

In addition, some waterways that do not appear as critical in normal times can become critical during flood events, as traffic is diverted when the main roads are flooded, and bridges become unusable. For example, the Dhaleshwari River near the Munshiganj launch terminal could become critical during flood events. Traffic at the Munshiganj launch terminal, the Sotaki launch *ghat*, and the Baherchar launch *ghat* could triple during flood events (TU Delft 2018).

GOVERNANCE OF THE LOGISTICS SECTOR

One of the defining characteristics of Bangladesh's logistics sector is the large number of institutions involved. An efficient multimodal logistics infrastructure network requires effective coordination in the planning, development, operation, and regulation of infrastructure. The extent of institutional fragmentation, coupled with overlapping mandates across institutions with potentially divergent interests and incentives, has led to poor coordination of Bangladesh's logistics sector. The limited effective capacity and integration of the infrastructure and its poor quality are consequences of this institutional structure.

To improve coordination and integrated planning across agencies and transport modes, in 2013 the Bangladesh cabinet approved the National Integrated Multimodal Transport Policy, which had been in the making for more than a decade. To date, however, the National Multimodal Transport Coordination Committee specified in the policy document has not been formed, and individual agencies have not made changes to their operating model.

Institutional fragmentation

Nine ministries have authority over the logistics sector in Bangladesh. In addition to the mode-specific ministries (the Ministry of Road Transport and Bridges, the Ministry of Railways, the Ministry of Shipping, and the Ministry of Civil Aviation), four other ministries have jurisdiction over logistics-related matters (figure 4.2). The Ministry of Local Government is responsible for rural roads, through its Local Government Engineering Department. The National Board of Revenue, under the Ministry of Finance, is the most influential regulatory body with respect to international logistics. It is responsible for administering tax and customs policy.

FIGURE 4.2

Institutions in Bangladesh's logistics sector

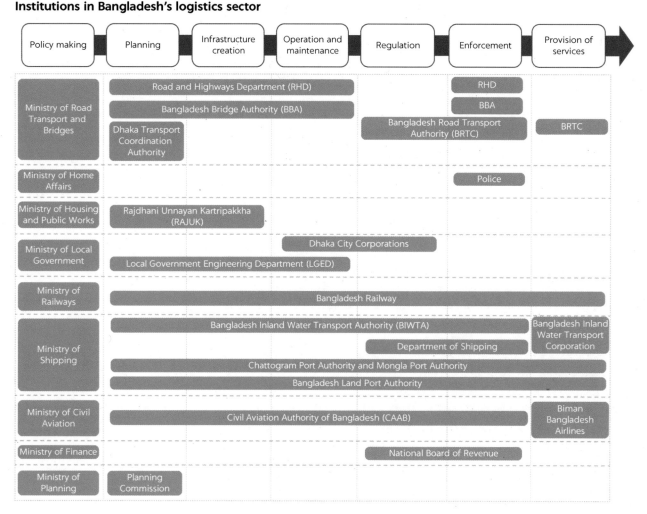

Source: PwC 2018.

Other high-level institutions, including the Bangladesh Planning Commission and the Public-Private Partnership Authority, also play key roles in the transport and logistics sector. The Bangladesh Planning Commission, under the Ministry of Planning, is responsible for short-, medium-, and long-term country-level plans as well as the approval of transport projects undertaken by transport organizations in various ministries. The Public-Private Partnership Authority, which is under the Prime Minister's Office, is responsible for identifying and facilitating infrastructure projects that can be developed under the public-private partnership mode.

Many subagencies are responsible for specific functions or geographic areas within given transport modes. In the road transport sector, for example, the Ministry of Road Transport and Bridges includes the Road and Highways Department (RHD), the Bangladesh Bridge Authority (BBA), the Bangladesh Road Transport Authority (BRTA), the Bangladesh Road Transport Corporation (BRTC), and the Dhaka Transport Coordination Authority (DTCA). RHD and BBA are the authorities primarily responsible for the planning, development, and maintenance of infrastructure. BRTA is responsible for regulating the sector. RHD is involved in enforcing BRTA regulations on overloading. DTCA is responsible for overall coordination of transport planning for all modes of transport in Dhaka city.

The division of responsibilities within a given ministry often creates complexity. For example, RHD is the chief institution tasked with planning, constructing, and maintaining major roads and bridges in Bangladesh. It is responsible for national highways, regional highways, and district roads as well as bridges that are less than 1.5 kilometers long. The BBA builds and maintains bridges longer than 1.5 kilometers. The two departments work independently, with minimal coordination on planning and implementation of projects. As a result, the capacity of bridges is not always commensurate with that of roads, creating bottlenecks to the movement of heavy trucks.

Overlapping mandates

Several institutions involved in the transport sector have overlapping responsibilities, with potentially diverging interests and incentives. In the road sector, for example, in addition to the RHD, the BBA, and the DTCA (in the case of Dhaka), the Local Government Engineering Department (LGED) and Rajdhani Unnayan Kartripakkha (RAJUK) have mandates on road infrastructure planning and construction. LGED is in charge of transport infrastructure in rural areas. It supposedly complements the RHD on subdistrict, union, and village roads, but it has also been involved in the planning and construction of primary and secondary roads and flyovers within the jurisdiction of the Dhaka City Corporation. RAJUK, in the Ministry of Housing and Public Works, is also mandated to take a leading role in road infrastructure, particularly the construction of roads linked to its own property development projects.

Overlapping mandates and shared ownership have made the planning, construction, and maintenance of transport infrastructure more complex than it should be. For example, eight flyovers have been built in Dhaka over the last decades, with the involvement of the five main agencies. Most of them were designed without paying sufficient attention to their integration in the surrounding road network or ongoing and committed projects along the same corridors (Bird and others 2018). In Chattogram access roads to the ports were developed without the inclusion of parking yards for trucks waiting to enter the port. As a result, trucks park on the roads or any other free space available in the city, causing congestion and delays.

Multiple authorities enforce road regulations. The traffic police are primarily responsible for enforcing the road-related regulations set by the BRTA, but the mobile courts introduced by the BRTA and the RHD carry out similar functions. The result is little regulation and more facilitation payments. The systematic use of facilitation payments increases the cost of operations and makes delivery times unpredictable and unreliable.

Inefficient planning and implementation

Lack of coherent planning for infrastructure development is the most important consequence of the institutional fragmentation and overlapping mandates in the transport sector. Although masterplan development and planning are underway for all transport modes, planning takes place within silos, with little effort to coordinate the development of the logistics network across the country. The planning gap has resulted in inadequate integration of modes to develop a truly multimodal transport network and concentration of freight movement on roads.

Transport planning in Bangladesh is inefficient not only because of the lack of integrated vision and coordination but also because of the limited capacity within individual agencies to undertake appropriate planning and prioritization (Planning Commission 2015). The RHD spreads its budget across an impractically large number of projects without proper prioritization, which results in inadequate budgetary planning of projects. For example, by the end of the Sixth Five-Year Plan, the RHD was funding 156 projects (Alam 2015). Insufficient budget allocation leads to implementation delays. For example, the upgrading of the Dhaka–Chattogram highway to a four-lane highway, which began in January 2006 and was to be completed by December 2013, was delayed by inadequate budget allocation (Alam 2015). The result is slow progress in filling the transport infrastructure gap across the board. The RHD and Bangladesh Railways did not achieve their physical targets during the Sixth Five-Year Plan (Planning Commission 2015).

A road masterplan and various policies—such as the National Land Transport Plan and the National Integrated Multimodal Transport Policy—which focuses on the maintenance of transport infrastructure exist, but implementation has been slow. Once projects are completed, there is no plan for maintaining the infrastructure. As a result, infrastructure deteriorates quickly and requires replacement before the end of its service life.

Robust planning and prioritization of transport infrastructure requires a good understanding of demand. Any demand analysis is only as good as the data it is based on. Bangladesh lacks good-quality data on transport demand for planning and prioritization (ADB 2012, Alam 2015). There is no origin-destination analysis for the entire country and hence no thorough understanding of commodity flows to inform the development of transport infrastructure to serve freight demand. The latest comprehensive inland water transport sector survey was carried out more than 20 years ago. Lack of updated economic parameters (on vehicle operating costs, for example) reduces the reliability of economic analysis of potential projects (Alam 2015, World Bank 2012). As a result, economic criteria are often ignored in setting expenditure priorities (World Bank 2012).

Weak enforcement of regulations

Weak enforcement of regulations defeats the purpose of regulation; it leads to inefficient use of and damage to infrastructure. One of the reasons for truck overloading is weak enforcement of overloading regulations. The BRTA is responsible for spotting whether modifications are made to accommodate overloading of cargo in the truck. Truck owners bypass this regulation by making facilitation payments to obtain fitness certificates. Trucks on the road get away with overloading because of inadequate controls. There are insufficient weighbridges across the country to control the loading of freight vehicles. Truck owners also reportedly make facilitation payments to traffic police and other monitoring authorities.

Protests from powerful groups often reduce the effective implementation of regulations. Under the latest regulations on vehicle weight limits, truck drivers were required to pay a fine of Tk 2,000 for overloading vehicles above the limits; repeated offenses were subject to fines of up to Tk 12,000. The government started enforcing the regulations, in August 2016. After protests from truck owners associations and drivers unions (including the burning of a weighbridge in Chattogram), the government deferred implementation of the regulations (Daily Star 2019). The government implemented axle-load regulations again in December 2017. New protests caused it to defer the implementation again. Although there may be some shortcomings in the regulation (as discussed below), the challenges faced by the government in enforcing the axle-load limits show its weak ability to enforce regulations.

PUBLIC FUNDING OF INFRASTRUCTURE

Bangladesh's infrastructure investment needs are significant, but there is limited fiscal space to fund them. Annual infrastructure investment needs are estimated to be as high as 10 percent of GDP, with transport infrastructure investment needs representing about half of it (Andres, Biller, and Herrera Dappe 2013; World Bank 2015). Public investment in infrastructure has been less than 2 percent of GDP for the last 15 years. The fiscal deficit, which increased from 3.5 percent of GDP in fiscal year 2014 to 4.5 percent of GDP in fiscal year 2018, remains below the 5 percent budget target because of continuous underimplementation of the annual development program (World Bank 2018).

The high cost of construction in Bangladesh exacerbates the challenges of limited availability of funding for new infrastructure. Bangladesh has significantly higher construction costs than other developing countries (figure 4.3). They reflect the high cost of imported inputs (paving materials, aggregates, stones, and structural steel) and geological factors. Governance issues in infrastructure construction, including poor planning and implementation, and corruption, are also key factors.

Without regular maintenance, infrastructure rapidly falls into disrepair, requiring expensive reconstruction to bring it back to adequate standards. The cost of full reconstruction of roads that have been poorly maintained averages at least three times the cost of maintenance (World Bank 2005). The build, neglect, and rebuild approach is thus extremely costly.

Even when funding for infrastructure is scarce, funds for new construction tend to be easier to obtain than funds for maintenance. The Bangladesh Parliament passed the Road Maintenance Fund Board Act in 2013 for the creation of a fund, under the RHD, for the maintenance, repair, and renovation of roads. The government has not yet made the fund functional, as its sources are still under consideration.

FIGURE 4.3

Cost of building roads in selected countries

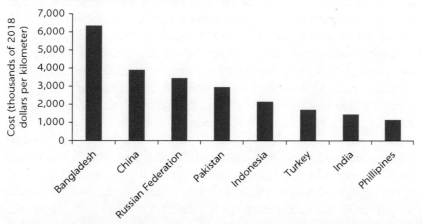

Source: Asian Infrastructure Investment Bank 2019.
Note: Costs are for a four-lane urban arterial road, including traffic-controlled intersections.

PRIVATE SECTOR PARTICIPATION IN INFRASTRUCTURE

The sheer size of Bangladesh's infrastructure investment needs provides an opportunity to rethink and improve the paradigm for providing transport infrastructure by giving the private sector a larger role to play in financing, managing, and operating infrastructure. Public-private partnership (PPP) is one modality for mobilizing the private sector for infrastructure provision. PPPs offer better value for money to public authorities by sharing risk with the private sector in the provision of public services. Other options, such as financing commercially viable state-owned enterprises and project finance, focus only on financing (ADB and others 2018).

PPPs in infrastructure are limited in Bangladesh, particularly in transport and logistics. Since 1990, 65 PPP projects were implemented, but they included just one airport project, two road projects, and three land port projects. The high risk associated with PPPs, because of the absence of efficient PPP framework and poor enforcement of contracts, has deterred private parties from participating in them. The PPP framework in Bangladesh is underdeveloped and lacks the appropriate contracting modalities to ensure effective risk sharing by public and private sector entities. The absence of such a framework reduces private sector confidence for executing PPP projects.

Bangladesh also faces challenges with regard to contract enforcement. It ranks second to last in enforcing contracts in the World Bank's *Doing Business*, considerably worse than neighboring countries India (which ranks 163th) and Sri Lanka (which ranks 164th) (World Bank 2019).[2] Resolving disputes takes more than 200 days longer in Bangladesh than in Sri Lanka. In Bangladesh the costs of court fees, attorney fees (where the use of attorneys is mandatory or common), and enforcement fees as a percentage of the claim value are more than twice as high as in India and almost three times as high as in Sri Lanka (figure 4.4, panel b). The poor quality of judicial processes in Bangladesh discourages private and foreign investors from investing in the country.

FIGURE 4.4

Doing Business in Bangladesh, India, and Sri Lanka

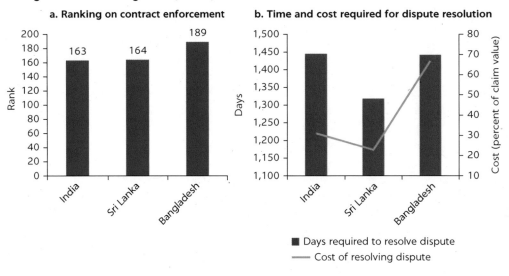

Source: World Bank 2019.

Successful PPPs in infrastructure require that (a) the government looks at PPPs as a source of efficiency, not of funding, and refrains from leaving the most complex, largest, and commercially unviable projects for the private sector; (b) the government takes on responsibilities and risks where it has the comparative advantage; and (c) the government carefully selects, designs, prepares, and oversees projects. Experience in South Asia and other parts of the world show that suboptimal risk allocation frameworks, tender strategies, and financing models can create incentives for bidders to be unrealistically optimistic, which can doom a program.

The development of a robust and effective PPP framework could address some of the challenges in each mode. Contracts for the operation and development of river terminals are awarded on an annual basis to private players. As the contract is for a single year, there is limited incentive to invest in the development of infrastructure. A PPP framework with longer concession periods could provide the assurance private operators need to invest in infrastructure development. PPPs in airport infrastructure and cargo handling are widely implemented around the world. They could solve the capacity and operational constraints facing the Hazrat Shahjalal International Airport. A well-designed PPP framework could bring significant efficiency gains, increase the quality of service, and generate enough revenues from user charges to compensate the private operator. An effective PPP framework for roads could help develop the corridors with substantial traffic.

Bangladesh is the only country on the Indian subcontinent in which the private sector does not play a meaningful role in the port sector. Globally, bringing the private sector into port operations has been a critical feature of port reform. The landlord port model is now viewed as best practice for port ownership and management structure. In this model, the government, often through a port authority, enters into an agreement with a private port operator or operators. The port authority acts as regulatory body and landlord, and private companies operate the port. Infrastructure is leased to private operating companies, who provide and maintain their own superstructure and own and operate the cargo-handling equipment. The ports of Chattogram and Mongla are the only ports on the Indian subcontinent that have not adopted this model. Both ports, particularly Chattogram, would benefit from participation of private players in the development and operation of terminals.

Mobilizing long-term private capital for infrastructure investment will require reforms beyond improving the PPP framework. Reforms in the banking sector and development of capital markets to create a more efficient financial sector are needed to mobilize long-term private capital for infrastructure investment (IMF 2018). The Bangladesh Investment Development Authority, the principal private investment promotion and facilitation agency in Bangladesh, has not included infrastructure in the list of permitted foreign investments. Foreign investors can provide financing for infrastructure investments only with prior approval from the government. Another deterrent to borrowing from a foreign lender is that the currency hedging market in Bangladesh is underdeveloped, increasing the risk of foreign funds. The hedging cost itself is comparatively high (at about 3.5 percent), and the market provides hedging for only a year. The commercial viability of state-owned enterprises (SOEs) needs to be strengthened to raise capital from financial markets. Transport and logistics SOEs continue to yield financial losses—Biman, the national airline is one of the main lossmakers—because of weaknesses in corporate governance (World Bank 2018).

POLICY AND REGULATORY RESTRICTIONS

Policy and regulatory challenges amplify inefficiencies in infrastructure. This section describes some of the policies and regulations that increase congestion and damage of infrastructure.

Construction of container freight stations

Bangladesh customs does not allow companies to open container freight stations at locations far from Chattogram Port. As a result, most bonded warehousing facilities are located or planned only in the Chattogram region. There is no container yard in Dhaka or its surrounding districts where importers can drop empty containers and exporters can pick up empty ones. As a result, importers (exporters) need to pay for the laden (empty) container movement from Chattogram Port to the factory premises. The empty (laden) container movement from the factory premises to off-dock or Chattogram Port reduces the incentive for inland containerized movement.

Containers as bonded items

Lack of empty containers is a major barrier to improving exports from river transport. Most empty containers in Dhaka are available at the Pangaon river terminal. Shippers wanting to export from other river terminals, such as Summit Alliance Port, need to source empty containers from Pangaon or from container freight stations in Chattogram. However, customs considers the empty containers bonded items; interterminal movements of empty containers are therefore deemed exports requiring prior customs approval. This regulation prohibits the free movement of containers between Pangaon and the Summit Alliance Port, which are next to each other, hindering development of container movement on inland waterways.

Lack of empty containers also hinders inland containerization. Importers must pay the custom duty on the value of the container if they want to bring the empty/laden container to the factory premises.

Commodity restrictions for custom clearance

Customs allows only 37 commodities to be cleared outside the port. About 95 percent of containers are therefore destuffed at Chattogram Port. Destuffing of containers at port leads to congestion inside the port. Once containers are destuffed, shippers prefer to use cargo vans to deliver their cargo instead of containers, which leads to an increase in the number of vehicles in the roads, as 1.25 covered vans are required to transport the cargo in one TEU container. The interaction of trailers with empty containers with city traffic adds to congestion within the city.

Shippers prefer to use cargo vans to transport imports and exports instead of containers for several reasons. First, there are no container yards outside the Chattogram region. Second, containers are treated as bonded goods. To protect containers from theft and any legal issues, shipping lines ask for an indemnity/bank guarantee from the freight forwarder, who passes on the cost to importers. For shipping lines, this practice hedges the risk of losing their container and protects against lawsuits, as this bond can be presented as a proof of custodianship of a container. Third, most ready-made garment factories are located away from main roads, in densely populated areas, where transporting containers is difficult. Factory layouts do not support the loading/unloading of containers inside the premises, as most manufacturing facilities are in four-story buildings that were not designed for the movement of heavy equipment.

Axle-load limits

Although the new rules are more liberalized than the old ones, the latest axle-load policy limits the maximum laden weight of a truck carrying a 20-foot container to 35 tons and the maximum laden weight of a truck carrying a 40-foot container to 44 tons. The average laden weight appears to stand at 37 tons for a 20-foot laden truck and 49 tons for a 40-foot laden truck, however. The latest axle-load regulations will thus increase the number of trucks on the road by hindering the movement of containerized cargo.

Although the axle-load regulations restrict the movement of container-laden trucks, they allow up to about 70 percent overloading in lower-category vehicles. The maximum permissible limit for a two-axle (six-tire) truck is 22 tons. A typical truck of this type manufactured by TATA has a maximum gross vehicle weight (including the weight of the cargo and the truck) of 16 tons, allowing for 7–9 tons of cargo. However, the latest axle-load regulations allow 13–15 tons of cargo weight to be hauled. This high a limit puts pressure on the road and bridge infrastructure and increases the risk of breakdown and accidents, undermining the safety of all road commuters as well as cargo.

Differential tax treatment favoring road transport

The provision of transport services for the movement of goods is subject to value added tax (VAT). For road transport, the VAT rates are 4.5 percent for the transport of petroleum and 10 percent for the transport of other goods, except fruits and vegetables, which are exempted. For transport service provided through inland waterways, the VAT rate is 15 percent. This differential taxation favors road transport over inland water transport. The Value Added Tax and Supplementary Duty Act, passed by parliament in 2012 but still not implemented, aims to create a level playing field with a uniform VAT rate of 15 percent for all transport modes. The government should refrain from setting different rates when implementing the VAT.

NOTES

1. About 72 kilometers between Laksam and Akhaura are expected to be converted to double track by 2020.
2. *Doing Business* measures the time and cost of resolving a commercial dispute and the quality of judicial processes.

REFERENCES

ADB (Asian Development Bank). 2012. *Capacity Building and Support to the Transport Sector Coordination Wing of the Planning Commission.* Manila.

ADB (Asian Development Bank), DfID (Department for International Development), JICA (Japan International Cooperation Agency), and the World Bank. 2018. *The Web of Transport Corridors in South Asia*. Washington, DC: World Bank.

Alam, G. M. K. 2015. "Strategy for Infrastructure Sector: Background Paper for the Seventh Five Year Plan." Policy Research Institute of Bangladesh, Dhaka.

Andres, L., D. Biller, and M. Herrera Dappe. 2013. *Reducing Poverty by Closing South Asia's Infrastructure Gap*. Washington, DC: World Bank.

Asian Infrastructure Investment Bank. 2019. *Asian Infrastructure Finance 2019*.

BanDuDeltAS. 2015. "Sustainable Transportation and Infrastructure." In *Bangladesh Delta Plan 2100 Formulation Project*. Bangladesh Planning Commission, General Economics Division, Dhaka.

Bangladesh Roads and Highways Department. 2018. *Maintenance and Rehabilitation Needs Report of 2018–2019 for RHD Paved Roads*. Dhaka.

Bird, J., Y. Li, H. Z. Rahman, M. Rama, and A. J. Venables. 2018. *Toward Great Dhaka: A New Urban Development Paradigm Eastward*. Directions in Development. Washington, DC: World Bank.

Daily Star. 2019. "Panel Formed to Set Weight Limits for Trucks on Highways." April 8. https://www.thedailystar.net/business/panel-formed-set-weight-limits-trucks-highways-1294174.

Gibson, A. 2015. "Enhancing Container Service in the Dhaka-Chattogram Corridor." Report prepared for the World Bank, Washington, DC.

HaskoningDHV. 2016. *Inland Waterway Navigability Improvement Feasibility Study: Early Assessment and Initial Prioritization Report*. Rotterdam.

IMF (International Monetary Fund). 2018. "Article IV Consultation Bangladesh." IMF Country Report 18/158, Washington, DC.

JICA (Japan International Cooperation Agency). 2017. *Preparatory Survey for Dhaka International Airport Expansion*.

Knight, Frank. 2017. "Mapping Report: Bangladesh Warehouse Industry." Background report commissioned by this study World Bank, Washington, DC.

Nyenrode Business Universitaet. 2014. *Exploring the Logistics Sector in Bangladesh: Opportunities, Threats and Practical information*. Breukelen, the Netherlands.

Planning Commission. 2015. *Seventh Five-Year Plan FY2016–FY2020*. Dhaka.

PwC. 2018. "Assessment of Freight Transport and Logistics Market in Bangladesh." Background report commissioned by this study, World Bank, Washinton, DC.

TU Delft. 2018. *Resilience of the Transport Network in Bangladesh: A Graph-Theoretical and Simulation Based Approach*. Report commissioned for a World Bank study, World Bank, Washington, DC.

World Bank. 2005. "Why Road Maintenance Is Important and How to Get It Done." Transport Note 4, Washington, DC.

——. 2012. *Building Institutional Capacity for Managing Bangladesh's National Road Network*. Washington, DC.

——. 2019. *Doing Business*. Washington, DC.

5 Logistics Services

INTRODUCTION

Demand for logistics services is centered in the Dhaka–Chattogram corridor, followed by three main corridors that largely serve the domestic market, as chapter 2 shows. International trade shipments form the bulk of the organized demand for logistics services along the Dhaka–Chattogram corridor. The three other major corridors connect Greater Dhaka with northwest, southwest, and northeast Bangladesh. The corridor connecting the northwest districts with Greater Dhaka facilitates the movement of agricultural products and the movement of export-import cargo destined for Nepal and Bhutan through the land ports of Banglabandha and Burimari. A third corridor connects Dhaka and Jeshore as well as the Benapole land customs station, through which most overland trade with India passes. A fourth corridor connects Dhaka and Sylhet. It facilitates the movement of consumption goods from the Dhaka and Chattogram regions to the northeast of Bangladesh. Together the four corridors generate a significant proportion of demand for logistics services in Bangladesh.

The quality and cost of logistics services depends on the market structure, regulation, trade and transport procedures, the broader business environment, and the infrastructure in place. This chapter assesses the logistics services sector in Bangladesh. It maps the range of services offered and the service provision models; assesses the quality of logistics services, the market structure, and challenges in the governance of the sector and the business environment; and discusses the potential for and barriers to regional integration of logistics services. The assessment draws on the findings of a survey of shippers and service providers across the country.

RANGE OF LOGISTICS SERVICES

The most common commercial logistics services—ranging from transport services to related ancillary logistics services, especially freight forwarding, customs clearance, and warehousing—are available in Bangladesh. The key to efficient services is how all the components function together, offering seamless services to shippers. In this respect Bangladesh's system is weak, as the system is largely fragmented, with each element offered as a separate service. The basic characteristics of each service are described below.

Transport services

Roads

Road transport is the dominant mode of transport in Bangladesh. A fleet of more than 190,000 trucks (BRTA 2018), with carrying capacity of 3–30 tons, is used to carry all types of goods.

The smallest vehicles, with a carrying capacity up to three tons, are used mostly for the short-haul movement of cargo within cities or districts or between adjoining districts. Unlike larger vehicles, these light trucks are allowed to enter Dhaka during the day. This is one reason why manufacturing companies make extensive use of light trucks to deliver goods locally and distribute their finished products. The next category of trucks carries 5–10 tons. These trucks are used to ferry export-import shipments of manufacturing industries, especially ready-made garments, footwear, jute, and similar industries. Some medium trucks are used for the long-haul domestic movement of cargo. The larger ones are also used to deliver agricultural products, logs, and construction material, among other good.

A third category of truck carries up to 16 tons. These trucks are used to transport stones, metal products, and some agricultural products. The last category is prime movers with trailers, which have carrying capacity of up to 30 tons. Prime movers with trailers are used primarily to transport containers within Bangladesh, especially between Chattogram and the Dhaka region. Trucks with flat-bed trailers are also used to transport iron bars and rods.

Inland waterways

The second-most utilized mode of transport in Bangladesh is inland waterways. The country has a fleet of about 14,000 cargo vessels, including dry-cargo vessels; barges, tankers, and double-bottom vessels, used predominantly to transport petroleum products; and sand carriers. It also has a large number of cargo country boats. Country boats are informal; their importance is difficult to quantify. The latest figure estimates the number of country boats used for cargo at about 261,000 (World Bank 2007).

About 1,200 barge operators are registered with the Water Transport Cell, a barge owners association. Barge operations fall into two categories. Domestic shipments include bulk import commodities from Chattogram Port to inland ports and a nascent industry focusing on containers. Regional operations transport fly ash from India and are quite small. Country boats and some unregistered barges operate informally to transport construction materials, vegetables, raw jute, logs, and other raw materials for industries located near river terminals.

Rail

Bangladesh Railways is the only provider of rail transport services. It is involved mainly in the transport of bulk commodities across the country and containers from Chattogram Port to the inland container depot at Kamalapur in the Dhaka region. Rail transport dominates the movement of containerized traffic between Chattogram and Dhaka. The corridor accounts for more than a third of rail freight volumes.

Air

Bangladesh has three international airports (in Dhaka, Chattogram, and Jeshore). Only the Dhaka airport is used for air cargo. The major export-import industries using air transport are ready-made garments, machinery, electronics, frozen food, and pharmaceutical products. The major destinations and origins for export and import of air cargo are Europe, East Asia, the Middle East, and the United States. A few major international airline operators fly into Dhaka, including Emirates, Etihad Airways, Hong Kong Airlines, Cathay Pacific, and Qatar Airways. Nearly all of them offer air cargo freight movement by a mix of passenger aircrafts and dedicated freighters. Biman Bangladesh facilitates cargo movement to the Middle East. Consultations with shippers in Bangladesh indicate that there is limited demand for domestic air cargo shipments.

Sea

Bangladesh is highly dependent on sea transport for its exports and imports. Most international shipping lines operate at Chattogram Port; some shipping lines also call at Mongla Port, with lower frequency. The shipping lines provide feeder services at Chattogram Port from major transshipment hubs in South Asia (Colombo) and Southeast Asia (Singapore and Malaysia).

Fragmentation

Core infrastructure in Bangladesh covers all transport modes and transport services are provided in all modes, but the use of multimodal transport is extremely limited. About 91 percent of shippers surveyed reported few to almost no instances in which logistics service providers used multimodal transport to bring down the cost of transport (figure 5.1). The fact that only the public sector provides rail service limits the scope of multimodal transport the private sector can provide. Other constraints are discussed below.

FIGURE 5.1

Use of multimodal transport by logistics service providers in Bangladesh

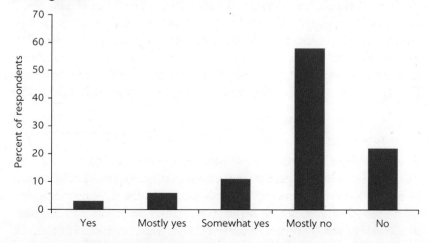

Source: Survey conducted for this report.

Warehousing

The market for commercial warehousing services is not fully developed. The level of outsourcing of storage and warehousing is very low. The sector is roughly organized into three categories: agricultural products (food grains and horticulture), imported manufacturing inputs and manufacturing outputs for export, and retail products. Dry agricultural and bonded warehousing are the most predominant types of warehousing.

Most dry agricultural facilities are owned by the government. These government-owned warehouses are under the control of the Directorate of Food. Distribution of grain is facilitated through a network of large silos, central storage depots, and local storage depots. Horticultural products are kept in cold storage warehouses distributed across the country. Potatoes are the key commodity stored in these warehouses. The cold stores operated by the state-owned Bangladesh Agriculture Development Corporation (BADC) are used to store potato seeds; private cold stores are used mainly to store potatoes.

The major operations of cold storage warehouses are unloading/loading, sorting, packing, and shuffling bags of about 85-kilogram capacity. Large cold storage warehouses benefit from large returns to scale, though the returns are not usually passed on to users. A major challenge faced by cold storage operators is fluctuations in the price of potatoes. When the price is too low, it is not profitable for traders or farmers to pay for storage and transport. They therefore abandon the product in the warehouses.

Import-export warehouses are used mainly to store containerized products. In addition to stuffing and destuffing containers, the facilities provide for the intermediate storage of goods (in container freight stations or bonded warehouses) before being loaded for exports or dispatched within the country.

Container freight stations are concentrated around Chattogram Port. Most facilities are operating at about 85 percent capacity utilization, because of restrictions on the licensing of new facilities near the port.[1] Tariffs for storing goods in container freight stations are set by the Bangladesh Inland Container Depot Association (BICA), in consultation with the Chattogram Port Authority (CPA). The charges for handling export containers are much lower than the charges for import containers, leaving container freight stations with little incentive to handle exports.

Bangladesh's retail industry consists primarily of small local outlets that store their merchandise in their shops. Some larger retail outlets may have a separate storage area designated for the storage of merchandise, which they maintain themselves.

Freight forwarding

Freight forwarders help organize inland transport, book space with sea carriers, and issue needed documentation. The industry is highly fragmented, with more than 2,500 freight forwarders operating in the country. The results of surveys conducted for this study indicate that a large number of small companies and individuals offer services out of their homes or small offices. These forwarders rely on local companies, small importers and exporters, or their associations with foreign vendors to generate business.

Most small-scale freight forwarders do not own assets; they rely on other providers to offer solutions. For example, trucking is sourced on the open market or from a known service provider. Customs clearance is handled by customs house agents. For storage, freight forwarders use off-dock facilities or inland container depots, where they consolidate and containerize cargo or pack and label it for export. Freight forwarders charge a commission of about Tk 3,500 per bill of lading.

A small but more developed class of freight forwarders have invested in their own facilities, such as transit warehouses for consolidating, packing, and labelling of cargo. They tend to be the few large multinational and domestic firms that provide the bulk of freight forwarding services in the country. They generate business through their overseas partner or network firms. Local business generation is limited for international firms. Some of the large forwarders in Bangladesh are Homebound, Agility Ltd., DAMCO, Kuehne Nagel, DHL, and EFL. One of the leading multinationals, Kuehne Nagel, handles about 45,000 TEUs a year, about 2.5 percent of total imports and exports of laden containers in Bangladesh. The other large operators handle about 35,000–45,000 TEUs a year.

Customs clearance

Customs clearance in Bangladesh is provided by customs house agents (CHAs). Most of the roughly 3,000 CHAs are individuals with clearing and forwarding licenses and three to four supporting staff. Many CHAs are standalone entities; others have ties to big firms, freight forwarders, or importers/exporters.

Typically, the CHA manages the entire custom clearance process. Under the process laid out by the National Board of Revenues, the CHA collects relevant documents and uploads them onto the customs system. Physical copies of the documents have to be submitted to the customs house. As the process is partly manual, some CHAs often pay facilitation fees to expedite clearance. After clearance, the CHA arranges with the importer to pay duties and taxes, after which the CHA liaises with a freight forwarder or, if he also provides forwarding services, organizes for final delivery of goods to the importer. CHAs charge based on the value of the consignment, typically 0.3–1 percent of the shipment value.

MODALITIES OF LOGISTICS SERVICES PROVISION

There are two main modalities for logistics services provision in Bangladesh, own-account operations and third-party or for-reward logistics provision. This categorization applies mainly to road and inland water transport services and warehousing, which firms can provide on their own or source from professional service providers. For rail, air, and sea shipping; freight forwarding; and custom clearance services, only third-party provision exists.

Own-account services

Own-account logistics services are often found in sectors that rely heavily on transport for delivering inputs or products or that require specialized vehicles. The relative sizes of own-account services and for-reward services differ across countries. Over the last 70 years, most advanced economies experienced a rapid expansion in for-reward operations, especially since the 1980s. In contrast, in many low-income economies, including Bangladesh, significant parts of the market rely on own-account services (Tanase and others 2016). Most large manufacturing firms in the country handle their transport and logistics requirements in house.

Own-account services in Bangladesh are associated with import-export sectors and firms involved in distribution within the country. These services serve a captive demand in the manufacturing and commoditized consumer goods sectors (mainly fast-moving consumer goods), which have to maintain high service levels to remain competitive. All major industrial firms—such as the Pran Group, Aarong Dairy, and the Bashundhara Group—maintain their own fleets of trucks, river vessels, and storage facilities. Some industrial groups have fairly large fleets of trucks. The Pran Group has the largest fleet in Bangladesh, with more than 1,500 trucks.

Manufacturing firms tend to maintain their own storage facilities, in order to store inventory needed to sustain their operations. The level of outsourcing of warehousing services is very low in the manufacturing industry. Many manufacturing firms maintain space within their own premises for the storage of materials and products. The storage requirements for distribution of finished goods are fulfilled through distribution warehouses maintained by manufacturing industries in high consumption regions.

The development of in-house logistics services in Bangladesh has been spurred partly by the lack of high-quality logistics service providers. One major downside is that own-account logistics services do not fully utilize assets. Unproductive or empty truck trips are common (Tanase and others 2016). In Bangladesh, it is conservatively estimated that 35 percent of all truck trips are running empty. Another downside is that Bangladesh's large companies and conglomerates are not generating the demand that would enable small commercial logistics service providers to grow. Small operators do not have access to some of the more lucrative segments of the market, which could incentivize them to modernize their fleets and operating practices. Table 5.1 summarizes the advantages and disadvantages of the two most common models for in-house provision of trucking services in Bangladesh.

Third-party services

Third-party logistics services are found in all regions of Bangladesh. They are most prevalent in regions that have a heavy concentration of industries, such as

TABLE 5.1 Advantages and disadvantages of in-house trucking services

OPERATING MODEL	ADVANTAGES	DISADVANTAGES
In-house use only (assets are owned or leased, drivers and crew are on payroll).	• Provides control over supply chain. • Improves reliability. • Allows flexible operations. • Allows firm to track and trace shipments. • Provides stable costing. • Allows firm to ensure that drivers and crew have right skills.	• Involves high incidence of empty running and therefore high costs. • Requires separate logistics department. • Creates redundant capacity during periods of low demand. • Slows pace of innovation. • Reduces size of for-reward services market.
In-house and for-reward for return trips (assets are owned or leased, drivers and crew are on contract, spot contracts for return trips).	• Provides some control over supply chain. • Reduces empty running, as for-reward services are offered if assets are not needed by primary user.	• Reduces reliability of service. • Reduces sector output, because of dearth of skilled drivers.

Dhaka and Chattogram. The organized for-reward fleet of river barges is used mainly to transport cargo from Chattogram to the rest of the country. The Water Transport Cell allocates cargo to barges on a first come first served basis. It sets the tariffs, preventing operators from competing on price. Access to the for-reward trucking services market is gained through a broker representing many service providers, through transport agencies, or by direct contracting between service providers and shippers.

Services through brokers

Small truck owners, with fleets of one to five trucks, depend on brokers for business. In this business model, brokers facilitate the provision of logistics services, acting as middlemen between shippers and service providers. Logistics services are provided on a spot contract basis. One broker can be an agent for several service providers. Brokers tend to be former truck drivers who have strong political backing and connections with drivers unions and associations. They have enormous influence over the functioning of the market and the setting of prices.

Arrangements that are intermediated by brokers represent the largest segment of the logistics services market in Bangladesh, especially in road transport. Agents, who are typically not professionally trained, interact directly with drivers, who do not always interact with customers. As a result, drivers are not always inclined to provide good-quality service, as strong drivers unions protect them from financial or disciplinary repercussions. Because owners do not interact directly with shippers, it is not possible for them to compete on quality of service.

In this model, shippers and freight forwarding agents inform the brokers of their transportation needs. Based on their experience and the demand–supply trends observed, the brokers quote a rate. Brokers operating in a particular market collude and fix the minimum threshold rates that can be charged to users for a particular route. Once enquiries have been made to the brokers, they interact with various truckers in the morning meetings at designated truck stands/markets to finalize the allocation of trips through a bidding process. Although the allocation of trips is carried out based on a bidding process, the benefits of this process—competitive quotes by truckers—do not translate into competitive prices for end users. Instead, brokers capture the benefits.

This model is used primarily by industries engaged in domestic commerce, as export-import industries demand reliable transport that this model cannot provide. It is more prevalent in regions such as Dhaka and Chattogram that have a continuous demand for transport services. The key truck stands in the Dhaka region are in Aminbazar, Gabtoli, Tejgaon, and Postogola. In the Chattogram region, the key truck terminals are in Kadamtali, Bandar, and Nimtola.

Services through agencies

Small to medium-size transport agencies (agencies with 10–50 trucks) that have direct relationships with shippers provide logistics services mostly on a spot contract basis. This business model is the most prevalent one used by small to medium-size transport agencies. These agencies have built their own fleets of vehicles and lease vehicles when required.

Transport agencies in this modality are members of various associations, such as the Truck Owners Association and the Covered Van Owners Association. Shippers contact these transporters directly or through their associations/ unions. Transporters cannot charge prices below the minimum threshold rates determined by the associations/unions.

Some transporters also enter into long-term contracts with shippers. The number of such contracts is very limited, however, because of the high prices charged. Drivers unions force transporters to inflate the prices for long-term contracts to accommodate price fluctuations during peak and festival seasons.

Service providers and shippers who interact through associations have limited control over the quality of services, as drivers, most of whom are low skilled and illiterate, become the most influential determinant of the service provided. This model is prevalent in the Dhaka–Chattogram corridor serving international trade traffic. Field assessments suggest that some operators have the potential to graduate to contract-type arrangements with large shippers.

Direct contracting between service providers and shippers

A few service providers with large enough capacity have direct relationships with shippers through long-term contracts (typically more than three months to up to three years). The providers offer services at pre-agreed upon rates, capacity, and reliability. The provision of transport services in such cases is facilitated through direct interactions between user industries and service providers. Operators are able to invest in technology, fleet renewal, and driver training to deliver better-quality services. One example is a company that caters to the entire distribution network of the British American Tobacco, one of the largest-volume shippers in Bangladesh. The company offers a wide variety of services, including warehousing.

Local players dominate the long-term contract segment of the market. International service providers and third-part logistics companies could enter this market, but the market is small and there are regulatory limits on direct entry (foreign operators have to form joint ventures with local companies).

Table 5.2 summarizes the advantages and disadvantages of the three most common models for for-reward provision of trucking services in Bangladesh.

INTEGRATION OF LOGISTICS SERVICES

The basic elements of a modern logistics system exist in Bangladesh, but logistics services are highly fragmented. Shippers typically work with more than one service provider to complete each shipment (figure 5.2). Most logistics service providers are active in only one service category of logistics. Only a few players offer combined services covering customs clearance, freight forwarding, and warehousing. Many of the nascent integrated services are along the corridors that generate consistent transport demand.

Very few domestic companies provide vertically integrated services. Most service providers run as almost informal enterprises and have low standards. Even many large freight forwarders do not offer integrated services. Multinational players such as Unilever and Nestlé therefore award separate contracts for transport, warehousing, and freight forwarding services.

TABLE 5.2 **Advantages and disadvantages of for-reward trucking services**

OPERATING MODEL	ADVANTAGES	DISADVANTAGES
Services through brokers (firm owns no assets, drivers are on contract, spot contracting only)	• No significant fixed costs for shippers.	• Drivers unions have greater bargaining power than truck owners. • Brokers have market power. • Owner has no relationship with customers. • Too few skilled drivers are available. • Quality of services is very low. • Business is run on mutual trust basis; no documents are signed. • Drivers overload trucks. • Shippers face problems related to availability of vehicles and price fluctuations.
Services through agencies (firms own and lease assets, drivers are on contract, mostly spot contracting)	• No significant fixed costs for shippers.	• Associations fix daily tariffs, which are subject to fluctuation. • Service providers have market power through associations. • Providers have no long-term relationship with customers. • Drivers are hired on contract, which reduces reliability. • Too few skilled drivers are available. • Investment in modern technology is limited. • Limited attention is paid to quality of service.
Direct contracts between operators and shippers (firms own and lease assets, drivers are on company payroll, long-term contracts)	• No significant fixed costs for shippers. • Long-term contracts provide greater business certainty, which allows operators to expand. • Customers are willing to pay premiums for improved service, which enables operators to invest in modern technologies. • Long-term contracts ensure availability of supply when needed and smooths price fluctuations. • Crews are provided with training, which improves their performance.	• Small size of market for premium services limits scope for growth.

FIGURE 5.2

Number of service providers per shipment in Bangladesh

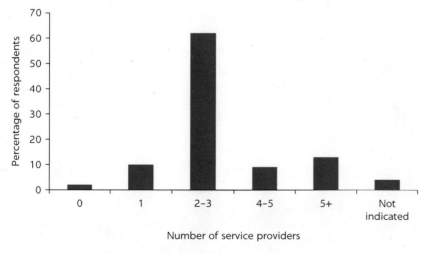

Source: Survey conducted for this report.

Partly because of the costs of coordination across several service providers, large firms in Bangladesh provide their basic needs in house.

International operators often find it difficult to compete in the market. In many countries, international players often take the lead in introducing innovative integrated logistics services. In Bangladesh multinational players that are willing to enter the market have to create a joint venture with a local company. Most local companies operating do not have the experience or expertise required to maintain high quality standards, and multinationals are not willing to form joint ventures with players that are not able to meet their standards.

QUALITY OF LOGISTICS SERVICES

Logistics services in Bangladesh are characterized by poor reliability, informality, the use of facilitation payments, poor skills, and limited use of the information technology (IT) tools that are increasingly prevalent in many other countries. Taken together, these characteristics indicate poor-quality services.

Poor reliability affects nearly all parts of the system. Seventy percent of shippers surveyed reported that delays in shipments are common (figure 5.3). More than 80 percent attributed delays in shipments to the poor condition of roads and congestion. Other reasons include regulatory controls (especially customs clearance) and the poor skills and lack of professionalism of operators and drivers. These results reflect insufficient capacity and poor operations and maintenance of infrastructure, limited intermodal integration, and the poor condition of the existing infrastructure (discussed in chapter 4).

Eighty percent of shippers surveyed reported instances of unprofessional behavior by logistics service providers (figure 5.4, panel a). More than 40 percent reported instances of manual error by logistics service providers (figure 5.4, panel b). About 90 percent of shippers surveyed reported that logistics service providers do not follow well-defined timelines and procedures for handling requests (figure 5.4, panel c). One of the reasons for low skills is the limited facilities for training and certifying manpower involved in logistics operations.

The low skills of logistics service providers increase logistics costs and the costs of externalities. In addition to reducing service quality, poor driving skills contribute to accidents, which add about 11 percent to the costs of operating trucking services. It is not unusual for logistics service providers, such as freight

FIGURE 5.3

Proportion of shippers reporting delays with shipments in Bangladesh

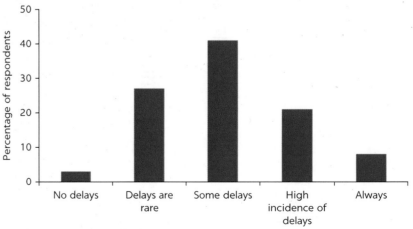

Source: Survey conducted for this report.

FIGURE 5.4

Shippers' perceptions of skill levels of logistics service providers in Bangladesh

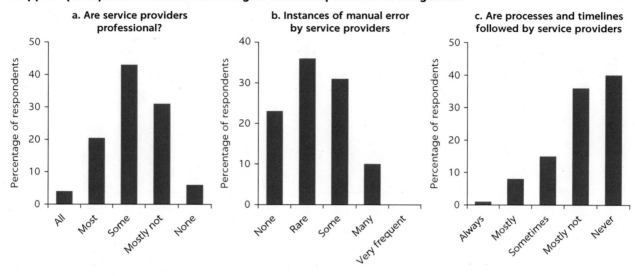

Source: Survey conducted for this report.

forwarders to manage the ground handling of their goods at the airport to expedite the process, because Biman (the ground handling operator) lacks the skilled manpower to handle cargo. They still have to pay Biman for service, however, increasing operating costs.

Logistics service providers lack adequate equipment. More than 90 percent of shippers surveyed reported that trucks are not in good conditions (figure 5.5, panel a). About 70 percent of shippers reported that logistics service providers do not have the required technology and assets to meet special cargo handling requirements (figure 5.5, panel b). The Dhaka–Chattogram route is dominated by trucks that carry up to seven tons of cargo. In other countries, a corridor with as much volume as the Dhaka–Chattogram corridor would be served by trucks with greater carrying capacity, including trucks carrying containers.

The lack of adequate inland water transport handling infrastructure and equipment results in delays, reducing the utilization and profitability of barge operators. Barge operators are dependent on manual laborers to load and unload barges, as most river ports do not have mechanized handling facilities. Contractors often provide fewer workers than necessary, further delaying the process.

The cargo handling equipment at Dhaka airport is insufficient to handle the level of traffic. Airlines often have to wait for equipment to load and unload cargo. Freight forwarders and airlines sometimes end up using their own manpower for handling and loading of export cargo; import cargo is handled only by Biman Bangladesh employees. The dispatch process at the airport is very slow. About 1,000 tons of cargo is unloaded daily, but the daily dispatch is about 300 tons a day (just 150 tons a day on Fridays and Saturdays). The delay in dispatch of imported goods increases the lead time for procurement of raw materials, increasing inventory costs.

Use of IT in the logistics industry is limited. There is very little tracking and tracing of shipments (figure 5.6), a capability that is common in

FIGURE 5.5

Shippers' perceptions of adequacy of equipment in Bangladesh

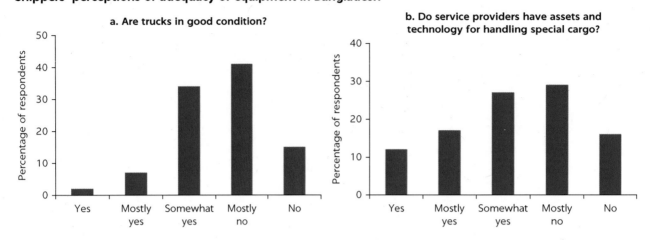

Source: Survey conducted for this report.

FIGURE 5.6

Shippers' perceptions of availability of tracking and tracing of shipments in Bangladesh

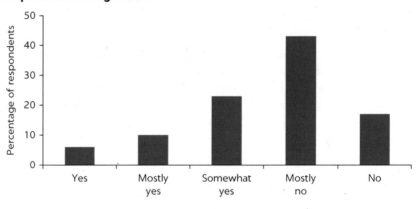

Source: Survey conducted for this report.

logistics management in many middle- and high-income economies. Poor use of IT in port logistics is emblematic of the poor use of IT across the logistics sector in Bangladesh and results in very little supply chain visibility for shippers.

The custom clearance process at land ports is a major bottleneck, as manual screening of cargo is done after cargo is unloaded at bonded warehouses, partly because of the lack of vehicle scanning machines. It typically takes 5–10 days for customs inspectors to complete the physical assessment of imported cargo. IT infrastructure to facilitate communication among various departments operating at the port, such as the Border Guards Bangladesh, the Land Port Authority, and the National Bureau of Revenue is lacking. Paper documents must be moved from one department to another, adding to the clearance time of cargo and encouraging facilitation payments to clear goods more quickly.

FIGURE 5.7

Shippers' perceptions of correspondence between quality and prices of logistics services in Bangladesh

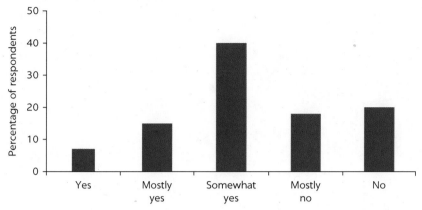

Source: Survey conducted for this report.

The prices of logistics services are high, especially given their poor quality. The low quality of logistics services leads to high logistics costs, as a result of delays, damage and loss of cargo, and actions to cope with it, such as higher inventory holding. More than three-quarters of shippers in Bangladesh consider the prices for logistics services to be higher than the quality of service warrants (figure 5.7), further increasing logistics costs. The main reason for the low quality–high price equilibrium in Bangladesh is the market structure, which is discussed in the next section.

DISTORTION OF LOGISTICS MARKETS BY UNIONS AND ASSOCIATIONS

In theory, Bangladesh's logistics services markets are contested. A large number of operators offer different types of services. All segments of the logistics services sector exhibit very low levels of market concentration. Thousands of single-vehicle operators offer road transport services, for example.

The large number of market players should nurture competition, but unions and associations interfere with the market mechanism and prevent full competition. The strong role unions and associations play in tariff setting and trip booking distorts market operations. More than 85 percent of shippers interviewed believe there is no competition in logistics service markets in Bangladesh (figure 5.8).

Drivers unions and owners associations distort market operations. They play a major role in allocating cargo to their members and fixing tariffs, which results in inefficient market operations. For instance, the Water Transport Cell, a legally constituted barge owners association, allocates imported cargo on a first come first served basis at fixed tariffs out of Chattogram Port. Even where there is direct contracting between service providers and shippers, drivers unions can affect prices. They do so when service providers outsource the operation of their trucks to third-party drivers who belong to the drivers union. When brokers establish that the prices quoted by a service provider are lower than the rates prevalent

FIGURE 5.8

Shippers' perceptions of competition in logistics service markets in Bangladesh

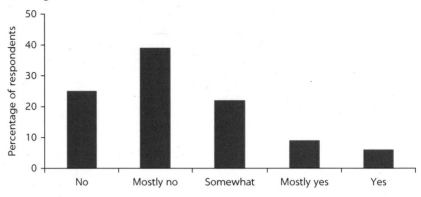

Source: Survey conducted for this report.

in the market, they force the drivers to refuse to operate the trucks of the service provider. Service providers are thus forced to quote prices in line with the prices prevalent in the market as decided by the brokers. In essence, unions and associations control access to loads and set prices above long-run marginal cost.

The involvement of unions and associations has several negative consequences. It disincentivizes provision of good-quality services and innovation, encourages on-account service provision, and limits the entry of international service providers. Trucking and inland water transport companies have no incentive to compete by offering higher-quality services, as they are not remunerated based on the quality of their services. As a result, companies have no incentive to innovate. Many large manufacturing companies operate their own fleets to better control their supply chains, at a higher cost.

The role that associations, agents, and drivers play in controlling access to loads also hinders the entry of international operators. International operators are not able to penetrate the market unless they work with local players who belong to unions and associations. Having to work with local players means that international operators do not have control over the quality of their services or the prices they charge. Labor unions and associations have enormous political influence and can dictate terms to multinational operators.

Unions and associations justify their existence by claiming that they protect drivers and owners by ensuring that everyone has cargo to transport and earn a living. However, the restriction to competition hurts both the economy as a whole (through higher transport costs and inefficient capital allocation) as well as drivers and owners. Truck owners could earn higher profits by merging and providing better-quality services, which would expand their businesses and even allow some of them to provide vertically integrated logistics services. Higher productivity of trucking and logistics companies would translate into higher wages for drivers.

Drivers unions and owners associations are large enough and well organized enough that they exert significant influence over policy reforms and market operations. For example, whenever the regulatory authority tries to set axle-load restrictions with severe penalties for overloading, the drivers union and associations call strikes to get the restrictions rescinded.

Reforms to curb drivers unions and owners associations power have been stalled. In 2012 the government enacted a Competition Act that aims to curb anticompetitive behavior in markets. The act aims to prevent collusion in the market and price fixing by industry players through various mechanisms, such as bid rigging, control of supply of goods or services, and abuse of dominant position. However, the act has not yet been fully implemented, and the Bangladesh Competition Commission stipulated in the act is not yet functional.

CHALLENGES IN *DOING BUSINESS* ENVIRONMENT

The role of drivers unions and owners associations is the most important obstacle to upgrading logistics services. The weak business environment is another important hurdle. In 2018 Bangladesh ranked 176th out 190 countries in ease of doing business in the World Bank's *Doing Business* report. Two important hurdles are related to access to credit (161st) and paying taxes (151st) (World Bank 2019).

Although the logistics sector in Bangladesh is open, especially to local investors, a common challenge faced by service providers is the lack of access to financing. Bangladesh's financial sector considers the road and inland water transport services sector risky and offers only limited and costly options for financing for-reward fleets. The risks largely reflect the mobile nature of the assets and the informality of the sector. The banking sector in Bangladesh extends credit facilities to reputable manufacturing companies for the purchase of trucks and river vessels for their own use.

The banking sector in Bangladesh refrains from extending credit facilities to for-reward trucking service providers for the purchase of assets because of the informality of the sector and the perceived lack of credibility. Risks are compounded by the fact that truck owners tend not to insure their trucks, which can result in total losses in the event of accidents. Rather than seek financing from banks, some truck operators access financing through truck dealers. The dealers and the banks financing them register the vehicles under their name and lend the trucks to purchasers to minimize losses. This financing often costs 2–3 percentage points more than the rates charged by public or private sector banks.

The inland water transport sector has fewer options than road transport. Banks provide only term loans, which they extend only to established barge owners with good credit history. Individual barge owners with one to two barges are unlikely to obtain loans from banks. Purchasers must put down a large deposit (typically 50 percent) along with a collateral of 100 percent of the loan value in the form of land, real state, and fixed deposits. The entry barrier to organized barge operators is thus high. The operating environment favors incumbent operators, who have established relationships.

Financing for the warehousing sector is easier than for transport sector. Banks provide loans to cold storages for agriculture products and custom-bonded warehouses—sectors the government considers priority sectors. One scheme is the Investment Promotion and Financing Facility, under which banks finance up to 75 percent of the project requirement.

Under Bangladesh's tax system for road transportation, organized logistics service providers pay higher taxes than do small informal players. The corporate tax rate for private limited companies is 35 percent. According to the National

Board of Revenues, tax avoidance and tax evasion are high in the unorganized transport services sector. It is more difficult to avoid the advanced income tax (AIT) than the annual individual and corporate income tax, as AIT payment is required at the time of issuance of fitness certificate. Small service providers tend to pay only AIT and have limited incentives to grow and become formal service providers.

CHALLENGES ASSOCIATED WITH THE GOVERNANCE OF LOGISTICS SERVICES

The need to develop a conducive institutional, policy, and regulatory framework in Bangladesh has long been identified (World Bank 1991). The institutional fragmentation in the logistics sector is related not only to infrastructure but also to services. At least 20 government agencies play a role in the regulation, provision, and operation of logistics services. Governance of logistics services also suffers from inadequate and outdated policies and regulations, including lack of integrated policy; a complex regulatory environment lacking in transparency; and weak enforcement of regulations.

One of the most important weaknesses in the policies in place is that they do not focus on services. The IMTP aims to establish an integrated approach to the development of different modes of transport and to promote multimodal operations in order to reduce transport costs and increase export competitiveness. The formulation of the IMTP represented a step toward development of the transport sector, but it does not focus on improving service quality in the logistics sector. The IMTP and NLTP focus mainly on the development of infrastructure for various subsectors. Both seek to increase private sector participation in the development of infrastructure but not in the provision of services. Only the public sector currently provides rail service, for example. The national-level policies developed by many other countries address improvement in infrastructure, integration of various modes of transport, and improvement in the quality of services.

Some elements of the regulatory environment for logistics services are outdated. The Motor Vehicle Acts, though amended from time to time through administrative orders, dates back to 1940. Customs handling, clearing, and forwarding are regulated under the Customs Act of 1969 and the Customs Rules and Freight Forwarding (Licensing and Operations) Rules 2008, which was updated in 2016. Warehousing is governed by a 1959 act that has not been updated and was drafted mainly for the storage of agricultural products.

Elements of the regulatory environment for logistics services are also patchy. Over time, as manufacturing expanded and industrial warehousing became more important, Bangladesh enacted regulations for bonded warehousing. As many as 320 acts, statutory rules and orders, meeting minutes, and instructions govern bonded warehousing. They are biased toward customs and exchange controls. As a result, the regulatory framework for industrial warehousing has important gaps, especially for safety. Many legal instruments are published online, but others are not readily available. Operations are governed by a patchwork of paper-based regimes and characterized by wholesale transaction-by-transaction control rather than modern approaches designed to promote efficiency.

Overall, Bangladesh has one of the most liberal investment regimes in South Asia (Nyenrode Business Universiteit 2014). But regulations are adopted from time to time to control access to parts of the services markets. For instance, the National Board of Revenues restricts the participation of foreign freight forwarders through statutory regulatory orders, which may not be in line with the industrial policy for the sector. In 2016 it amended the Freight Forwarding (Licensing and Operations) Rules 2008 to limit international logistics service providers from providing freight forwarding services in Bangladesh. As a result, the share of international firms in joint ventures fell from 49 percent to 40 percent. Although the restrictions are on freight forwarding, they affect the entire logistics industry, contributing to the fragmentation of the logistics sector and the slow pace of modernization.

According to the Customs Act, 100 percent foreign-owned companies cannot be granted customs handling licenses. A foreign company must enter into a joint venture with a local company, and foreign ownership may not exceed 40 percent. Customs handling agents also need to join the clearing and forwarding associations. To provide forwarding of air freight, companies must obtain a separate air freight forwarding license from the Civil Aviation Authority Board. These limits on foreign ownership impede the transfer of knowledge.

Weak enforcement of regulations defeats the purpose of regulation and results in poor service. Unqualified drivers driving heavy motor vehicles pay facilitation payments to obtain licenses. Modified or unfit trucks are issued fitness certificates. These practices have resulted in increases in the number of unskilled drivers and substandard trucks on the road. In water transport, just four surveyors at the Department of Shipping are responsible for inspecting more than 10,000 vessels and issuing fitness certificates. As a result, certificates are issued without proper inspection, following the payment of facilitation payments, compromising the safety of vessels and the quality of services. Corruption is very high, with facilitation payments institutionalized in the system.

POTENTIAL OF AND BARRIERS TO REGIONAL INTEGRATION OF LOGISTICS SERVICES

Bangladesh is in one of the most economically dynamic regions in the world. However, it is the world's least integrated region (Rahmatullah 2006). There is huge potential to benefit from enhanced trade integration. Exploiting that potential requires addressing both trade policy and logistics constraints.

Among the constraints to overland trade are restrictions on products that can be traded through particular check posts (so-called port restrictions) (Kathuria 2018). Negotiations have been ongoing since 2014 to lift restrictions on trade through certain posts between Bangladesh and India. Measures are also needed to harmonize and standardize policies and procedures for cross-border provision of logistics services.

Bangladesh could serve as a transit point for trade between northeast India and the rest of India, as well as for trade between Nepal and Bhutan and other countries. The absence of integrated and modern transit regimes has long been an impediment to the flow of freight traffic across South Asia, however. Bangladesh does not permit vehicles from neighboring countries to cross its borders. Goods therefore have to be offloaded at the border and transferred to

Bangladeshi trucks. The same wasteful procedure affects railways: Freight is taken off one train and put on another to cross the border. The governments of India and Bangladesh have been discussing how Indian traffic can cross from the rest of India to the northeast states across Bangladesh. The intention is primarily to allow traffic between western Bengal and the landlocked Indian states in the northeast. Doing so would halve the travel distance to about 500 kilometers.

Bangladesh is party to several regional and international agreements that affect freight transport and logistics. Some of the most important agreements are the 2015 Bangladesh-Bhutan-India-Nepal Motor Vehicles Framework Agreement for the Regulation of Passenger, Personal, and Cargo Vehicular Traffic (MVA), which was signed under the South Asian Association for regional Cooperation (SAARC); the June 2015 agreement on Coastal Shipping between Bangladesh and India; and the renewed Protocol on Inland Water Transit and Trade (PIWTT). The MVA lifts many restrictions on cross-border road transit for vehicles, passengers, and cargo across the territories of the countries. The agreement on coastal shipping allows goods to move by sea from the eastern seaports of India to Chattogram Port. The PIWTT contains new trade facilitation measures and additional ports of call on the inland waterway transport system. Other bilateral and multilateral agreements encompass cross-border transit by road, rail, and inland waterways.

These agreements are important for improving logistics performance, as they can be used to set minimum standards that participating states should comply with to allow smoother operation of cross-border transport services. They include the exchange of traffic rights, standards for the development of infrastructure and its interconnectivity, the development of customs and related border management infrastructure and systems, and the streamlining of processes and priorities for further development of systems for regional connectivity.

A functional transit system between the countries of South Asia and between South Asia and the Association of Southeast Asian Nations (ASEAN) has the potential to transform the trade facilitation environment in the region, especially in the landlocked countries. The problem is a very specific one that requires a practical transit solution on a few identified road corridors with significant traffic potential. This solution needs to include at least two features. First, it needs to create a functional transit procedure through Bangladesh that would allow seamless movement of goods between western Bengal and the northeast states of India, with no inspections en route or at the border and no transloading at the border. Second, it needs to include mechanisms for Bangladesh to recoup the costs associated with required infrastructure and services, based on universal principles of freedom of transit.

The ongoing and planned improvements in intra- and interregional connectivity are adding to the urgency of agreeing on such regimes. Several international practices can be drawn on. The leading global instrument for transit is the United Nations Transports Internationaux Routiers (TIR) Convention, which India ratified in 2017 (Bangladesh has not yet done so). One of the likely benefits of joining the TIR would be the potential spillover effects across the region. Landlocked Bhutan and Nepal need access to seaports and harmonized agreements to reduce time and costs by easing access to the ports of Bangladesh. A functional regional transit system is therefore an imperative for South Asia. Countries should also take advantage of the new capabilities offered by IT and data-sharing among customs administrations.

The efficiency of inland water transport also needs to be enhanced. Recent developments—such as the 2017 signing of a memorandum of understanding between Bangladesh and Bhutan on the use of inland waterways for bilateral trade and transit cargo and passenger movement on the coastal and PIWTT routes between India and Bangladesh—indicate that inland navigation is gaining traction in the Bay of Bengal subregion. The agreement between India and Bangladesh on the development of a fairway from Sirajganj to Daikhowa and Ashuganj to Zakiganj on the PIWTT would pave the way for year-round navigation of these routes. It should facilitate bilateral and transit trade, a large part of which will move through National Waterway 2 in India.

NOTE

1. A new regulation requires that any new facilities be outside a 20-kilometer radius of the port.

REFERENCES

BRTA (Bangladesh Road Transport Authority). 2018. Number of Registered Motor Vehicles. https://brta.portal.gov.bd/sites/default/files/files/brta.portal.gov.bd/monthly_report/d4d56177_644f_44f8_99c4_3417b3d7b0f4/MV_statistics-bangladesh-march-18.pdf.

Kathuria, S. 2018. *A Glass Half Full: The Promise of Regional Integration in South Asia.* Washington, DC: World Bank.

Nyenrode Business Universiteit. 2014. *Exploring the Logistics Sector in Bangladesh Opportunities, Threats and Practical Information.* Netherlands Bangladesh Business Platform, Utrecht.

Rahmatullah, M. 2010. "Transport Issues and Integration in South Asia." In *Promoting Cooperation in South Asia: Beyond SAFTA*, ed. S. Ahmed, S. Kelegama, and E. Ghani. Washington, DC: World Bank.

Tanase, V., C. Kunaka, N. Paustian, and P. Philipp. 2016. *Road Freight Transport Services Reform: Guiding Principles for Practitioners and Policy Makers.* Washington, DC: World Bank.

World Bank. 1991. *Bangladesh Transport Sector Review.* Washington, DC.

———. 2007. *People's Republic of Bangladesh Revival of Inland Water Transport: Options and Strategies.* Bangladesh Development Series Paper 20, Washington, DC.

———. 2011. *Connecting Landlocked Developing Countries to Markets. Trade Corridors in the 21st Century.* Washington, DC.

6 Impacts of More Efficient Logistics

INTRODUCTION

Improvements in transport infrastructure and services can better integrate Bangladesh with the rest of the world. The link between logistics costs and trade is clear: Better logistics performance leads to more trade, greater export diversification, increased attractiveness to foreign direct investment, and economic growth (Arvis and others 2012). Various inefficiencies have increased logistics costs in Bangladesh. Removing them could yield significant increases in trade. A percentage point reduction in transport costs could increase the demand for ready-made garments and textiles by 7.4 percentage points (Imbs and Mejean 2017).

Bangladesh's economic activity is highly concentrated in a small number of locations. Secondary cities and regions far from Greater Dhaka and the Chattogram metropolitan area struggle to attract firms and workers, particularly in export-oriented manufacturing. Greater Dhaka and Chattogram, with their disproportionate share of economic activity, suffer from higher land prices, congestion, and pollution. The balance between the benefits and costs of agglomeration is one of the factors determining the level of concentration around a few cities.[1] Differences in access to efficient transport infrastructure and services also explain why most export activities are in or around Dhaka and Chattogram.

Better integration with global markets through lower logistics costs would affect regions differently. The magnitude of improved market access; local comparative advantage (endowments of primary factors, technology, preferences); the mobility of people; and changes in technology that allow for scale and clustering determine how districts adjust. It is therefore important to understand the impact of different logistics interventions on the economic geography of Bangladesh. This chapter presents the results of a spatial general equilibrium model that was developed and calibrated for Bangladesh to assess the impacts of removing logistics inefficiencies.

EVALUATING LOGISTICS INTERVENTIONS WITH A GENERAL EQUILIBRIUM MODEL

Reductions in logistics costs affect the prices of goods, wages, and land rents, which drive workers' decision to migrate and firms' decisions about whether and where to produce. Lower logistics costs reduce the price of imports for consumers and increase the price local exporters receive. Production of exports increases in regions with lower logistics costs; if there are no frictions in the labor market, workers in the export sectors benefit from higher wages, which puts pressure on wages in nontradable sectors (manufacturing for domestic consumption and services). Because of higher wages and lower import prices, workers are attracted to regions that benefit from improvements in connectivity to global markets. The increased purchasing power of workers and the arrival of new workers increase the demand for nontradable goods and services. Regions that benefit from lower logistics costs become more crowded, competition for land becomes fiercer, and land prices increase. Nontradable sectors also face higher wages and land rents, which puts upward pressure on their prices. Higher prices for nontradables soften workers' incentives to move to a region. The effect of a reduction in logistics costs depends on all these forces.

Research in quantitative spatial economics mimics the behavior of firms and workers in deciding what, how much, and where to produce. Their decisions are reconciled through general equilibrium models that can be calibrated based on the observed level of variables such as population density and economic activity at each location. These models can be used to assess the effects of interventions that reduce logistics costs on the spatial distribution of economic activity.

The spatial general equilibrium model for Bangladesh assesses the effects of improvements in internal logistics on the integration of districts with global markets. It looks at how reductions in logistics costs affect the competitiveness of districts in the production of imports and exports (tradable goods). The model relies on work done on Argentina (Fajgelbaum and Redding 2018) and the Belt and Road Initiative in Central Asia (Lall and Lebrand 2019).

The model (described in detail in Herrera Dappe and Lebrand 2019) has three building blocks: geography, economic activity, and workers. They are connected by the goods prices, land rents, and wages in each district. Consistent with the idea of a general equilibrium, prices and wages adjust to balance supply and demand in each district.

Geography

The model allows for spatial granularity at the district level. Each of Bangladesh's 64 districts is characterized by its location, land area, livability, economic structure, and firm productivity. Livability captures the quality of life in a district, which is determined by factors such as the quality of education and health services. It influences where people chose to live. Economic structure refers to the share of employment in tradable and nontradable sectors in the district. Although production inputs are similar across districts, the productivity of firms differs, because of factors such as the infrastructure and technology available. The model assumes that Chattogram is the only coastal gateway in Bangladesh (in fact, it handles about 85 percent of trade). Mongla, the second-largest port, handles mostly imports.

Economic activity

Firms are classified as producing tradable or nontradable products. Given that ready-made garments represent 84 percent of the value of Bangladesh's exports, the model assumes that all exports are from that sector. The basket of imports is more diverse, including inputs for the garment sector and other sectors. The nontradable sector includes manufacturing for local consumption and services in general. The model considers tradable services as nontradable, because changes in transport costs to access Chattogram Port are unlikely to affect their production patterns. The model focuses on changes in employment in nonagricultural sectors.

Workers

Workers choose the sector in which they work and the place they live. All workers derive their income from employment and spend it on goods and service produced locally or imported. Workers' decisions on where to live and where to work depend on rents, wages, and livability across districts.

Calibration of the model

The information needed to calibrate the model comes from traditional data sources, such as surveys and geo-coded information on the transport network. Four types of data at the district level are used: land area, number of employees, sectoral shares of employees, and transport costs. Land area consists of used land units (cropland, irrigated, urban land) using the European Space Agency land categories from the Aiddata database (Defourny 2017). Employment levels and shares come from the 2013 Labor Force Survey, which provides estimates of employment in agriculture, ready-made garments, other manufacturing, and services.

Transport costs are measured as a function of the travel time to Chattogram Port from the center of each district. The travel time, which is calculated using GIS network techniques, is the shortest time given all possible routes in the road network. Travel times are based on actual speeds collected from more than 200 inter-city road segments across the country and random speed assignment to remaining segments based on distribution of speeds in nearby segments. Given the optimal transport times to reach Chattogram Port, logistics costs are parametrized based on the estimates presented in chapter 3.

ESTIMATING THE DISTRICT-LEVEL EFFECTS OF LOGISTICS INTERVENTIONS

Inefficiencies in transport and logistics are driving logistics costs. They include the congested and poor quality infrastructure; limited multimodal integration; the inefficient operation of infrastructure, particularly port infrastructure; limited competition in logistics services markets; the poor quality and integration of logistics services; the limited containerization of inland transport; the large number of empty trips; accidents; and facilitation payments. These inefficiencies lead to high direct and indirect (opportunity) costs.

Interventions to remove inefficiencies can have different effects on economic geography, even if they yield similar reductions in logistics costs. Four scenarios are examined:

1. *Reducing dwell times at Chattogram Port.* This scenario assumes that dwell times at Chattogram Port decrease by one day.
2. *Improving logistics policies.* This scenario assumes that a set of policies to tackle the low quality of logistics services, facilitation payments, and other inefficiencies is implemented.
3. *Reducing congestion on national highways.* This scenario assumes that the minimum speed along national highways increases to 40 kilometers an hour.
4. *Adopting a comprehensive approach.* This scenario assumes that all the interventions in scenarios 1–3 are implemented together.

Effect of reducing dwell times at Chattogram Port

Container dwell times at Chattogram Port are very high—11 days for import containers and 4 days for export containers (HPC, Sellhorn Engineering, and KS Consultants 2015). Inefficient port operation, limited port and evacuation capacity, and lengthy clearance processes are some of the reasons for the high dwell times. Other inefficiencies in the logistics chain that lead shippers to use the port for storage also increase dwell times.

A one-day reduction in dwell times at Chattogram Port would increase Bangladesh's exports by 7.4 percent. Reducing dwell times by removing inefficiencies in the sector would reduce logistics costs for shippers across the country. It is assumed that a one-day reduction in dwell time reduces transport costs as share of sales by 1 percentage point (Hummels and Schaur 2011). Using the estimate by Imbs and Mejean (2017) of the elasticity of demand for imported textiles from Bangladesh's main trading partners, a 1 percentage point reduction in transport costs as share of sales would increase demand for Bangladesh's exports by 7.4 percent.

Reducing dwell times at Chattogram Port by one day would increase employment and raise real wages in Greater Dhaka and Chattogram. The reduction in logistics costs would leverage the comparative advantage of districts with already large shares of employment in ready-made garments, such as Gazipur, Dhaka, and Chattogram. The effect on the spatial distribution of economic activity would be to further concentrate it in and around the two largest urban areas (map 6.1, panel a). All districts, including districts in which employment would fall, would benefit from higher real wages, but real wages would increase significantly more in districts with large ready-made garment sectors (map 6.1, panel b). The increase in real wages is driven by lower prices of imports across districts and higher prices of exports net of logistics costs, which increase wages in the garment sector and put pressure on wages in other sectors, including the nontradable sector.

Effect of improving logistics policies

Interventions that do not reduce port dwell times but increase the quality of logistics services, and competition in logistics services markets; crack down on facilitation payments; and better match supply and demand to reduce empty trips would also reduce logistics costs. This scenario assumes that logistics costs

MAP 6.1

District-level changes in employment and real wages associated with a one-day reduction in dwell times at Chattogram Port

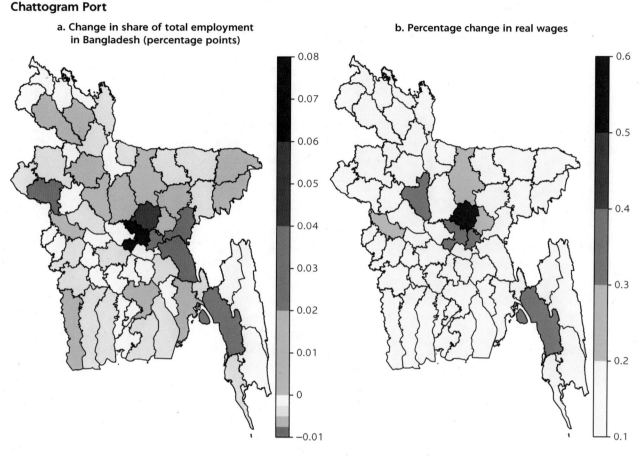

a. Change in share of total employment in Bangladesh (percentage points)

b. Percentage change in real wages

Source: World Bank analysis.

as a percentage of sales decrease by 1 point (or 17 percent of domestic logistics costs), which is equivalent to the cost reduction in the previous scenario to facilitate comparability. Bangladesh's exports would increase by 7.4 percent, the same increase associated with reducing port dwell time by one day.

National policies to reduce logistics costs increase economic activity in more districts than a reduction in port dwell times. Relative to the previous scenario, the concentration of employment increases slightly more in Greater Dhaka and decreases in Chattogram. Western districts such as Khulna, Kushtia, Kurigram, and Nilphamari increase their share of employment, thanks to national policies to reduce logistics costs (map 6.2, panel a). Policies that yield a uniform reduction in logistics costs across the country (that is, independent of the time it takes shippers to reach the port) leverage the comparative advantage of districts more than port-centric interventions.

Districts in and around Dhaka benefit the most, because they have a comparative advantage in ready-made garments and higher livability. Reductions in logistics costs only partly explain the effects of improved logistics on the ability of districts to attract workers (figure 6.1, panel a). Higher employment growth is observed in regions that experience significant reductions in logistics costs but also have a comparative advantage in producing export goods and are attractive locations for workers (figure 6.1). Except for Chattogram, where logistics costs

MAP 6.2

District-level changes in employment and real wages associated with logistics policies in Bangladesh

a. Change in share of total employment in Bangladesh (percentage points)

b. Percentage change in real wages

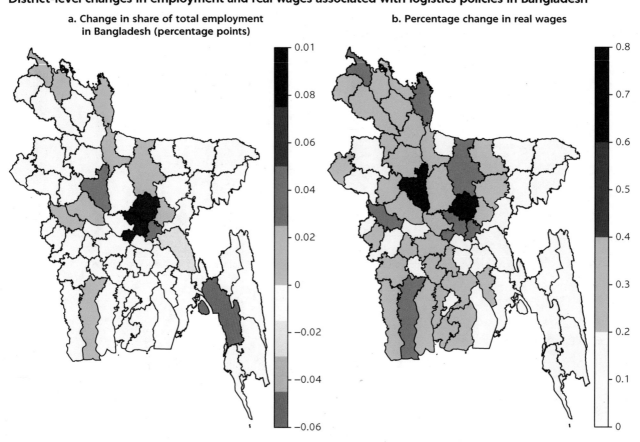

Source: World Bank analysis.

barely change, workers tend to move to districts that have the greatest comparative advantage in producing ready-made garments and livability. This finding suggests that other forces—such as labor market density, agglomeration gains, and access to education, health, and other services—are important and that complementary policies in these areas might increase the attractiveness of more distant districts.

Gains in real wages are slightly higher at the district level than in the previous scenario. Lower logistics costs improve accessibility to global markets, increasing export productivity and wages in the sector. The spatial pattern of real wage gains is different than in previous scenario, with workers in most districts far from Chattogram Port enjoying larger increases in real wages than workers in Chattogram and districts closer to it (map 6.2, panel b).

Effect of reducing congestion on national highways

Reducing congestion on the core road network would cut transport times to reach Chattogram Port, especially for shippers in districts that are far from the port. Congestion on inter-city roads is a serious problem in Bangladesh, with average speeds in several segments below 40 kilometers an hour. Congestion on the national highways network could be reduced by increasing road capacity,

FIGURE 6.1

Correlation between change in employment and logistics costs, initial employment share of ready-made garments, and livability in Bangladesh

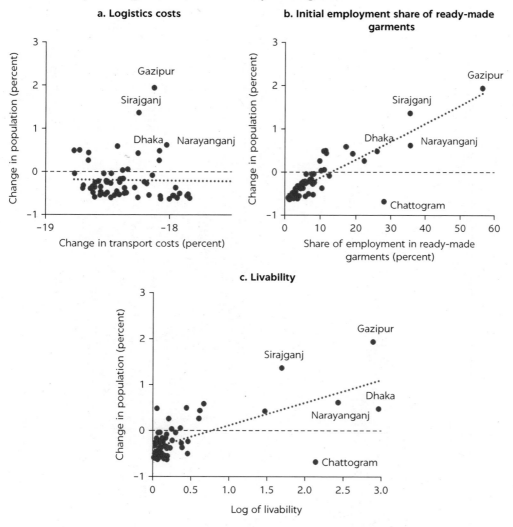

Source: World Bank analysis.

improving the quality of roads, shifting traffic from roads to railways and inland waterways along multimodal corridors, removing constraints to containerization and the use of bigger trucks, and reducing the number of empty trips, among others. Setting the minimum speed along national highways at 40 kilometers an hour would reduce logistics costs as a share of sales by 0.5 percentage points—half of the reduction in the previous two scenarios—increasing Bangladesh's exports by 3.7 percent.

Lower congestion on national highways would increase the concentration of employment in and around Dhaka. The reduction in travel times would reduce logistics costs, improving the accessibility of districts to global markets, with districts far away from Chattogram experiencing the largest reductions in logistics costs. Western districts such as Sirajganj and Kushtia would experience some of the largest employment growth rates, similar to or even larger than gains in Gazipur (map 6.3, panel a). Western districts start from a low employment base, however; more workers would move to Dhaka and Gazipur, which explains the

MAP 6.3

District-level employment effects of raising minimum speed on national highways to 40 kilometers an hour in Bangladesh

a. Change in number of workers (percent)

b. Change in share of total employment in Bangladesh (percentage points)

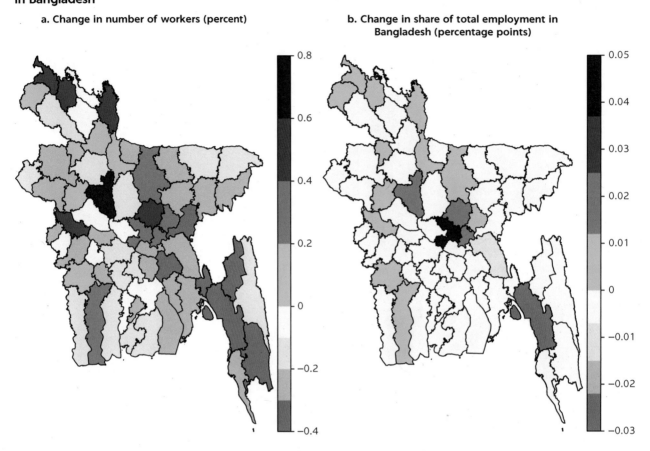

Source: World Bank analysis.

further concentration of employment in and around Dhaka district (map 6.3, panel b). Reducing congestion would increase the concentration of employment in and around Dhaka by much less than reducing dwell times at port.

Although some districts lose workers, real wages increase in all districts. Lower congestion along national roads reduces logistics costs for all districts, lowering imports prices, increasing the price ready-made garment exporters receive and raising real wages. The districts in which the percentage change in real wages are largest also experience the largest percentage growth in workers (map 6.4). Increasing the minimum speed on national highways to 40 kilometers an hour yields smaller increases in real wages than a one-day reduction in container dwell times at Chattogram Port.

Effect of adopting a comprehensive approach

Increasing the efficiency of the logistics sector requires a comprehensive approach that tackles delays at Chattogram Port, congestion along the road network, the low quality of logistics services, facilitation payments, and other inefficiencies. A comprehensive approach that combines all these interventions would reduce logistics costs as a share of sales for tradable goods by 2.6 percentage points.

MAP 6.4

District-level percentage change in real wages associated with increasing minimum speed on national highways to 40 kilometers an hour in Bangladesh

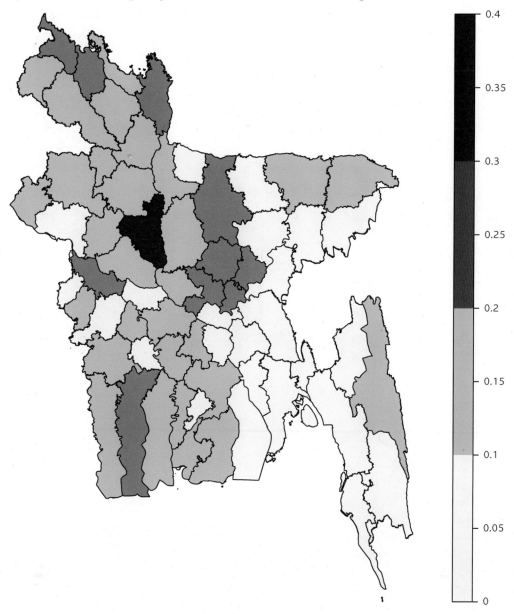

Source: World Bank analysis.

The decrease in logistics costs would yield a larger increase in exports and real wages across the country than in the previous scenarios and strengthen the primacy of Greater Dhaka. Bangladesh's exports would increase by 19 percent under the comprehensive set of interventions. The increase in the price of exports (net of transport costs) and the decrease in the price of imports would yield an increase in real wages of up to 1.6 percent, with workers in Gazipur enjoying the largest increase (figure 6.5, panel b). Workers in Dhaka, Narayanganj, Sirajganj, and Kushtia would also enjoy large increases in real wages.

MAP 6.5

District-level employment and wage effects of a comprehensive approach for increasing logistics efficiency in Bangladesh

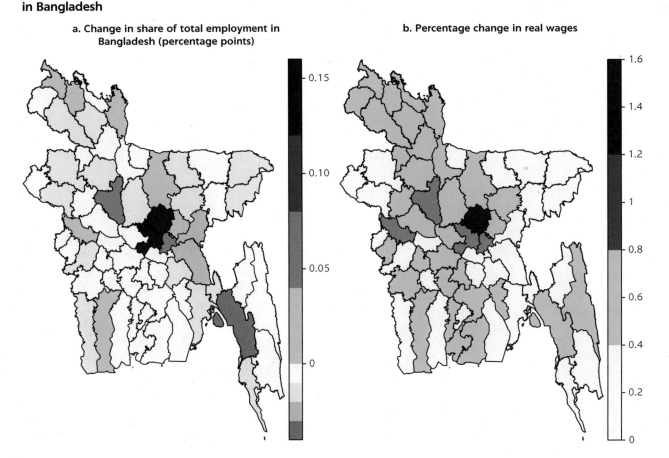

a. Change in share of total employment in Bangladesh (percentage points)

b. Percentage change in real wages

Source: World Bank analysis.

Combining the three sets of interventions would leverage the comparative advantage and livability of Dhaka and Gazipur in attracting employment more than in each of the previous scenarios. Eleven of the 64 districts would create jobs and attract workers from the rest of the country, increasing their share of total employment (figure 6.5, panel a). Dhaka and Gazipur, followed by Narayanganj and Sirajganj, would attract most of the economic activity. The results indicate that the logistics policies aimed at improving the quality of logistics services and the costs of those services are the predominant force behind the changes in the economic geography of Bangladesh. The horizontal nature of the interventions further leverages the advantages of Greater Dhaka over the rest of the country.

NOTE

1. Firms benefit from having suppliers and buyers close to each other and having access to a large pool of workers (agglomeration benefits), which leads to concentration. But high concentration of economic activity and population leads to congestion and pollution, decreasing the livability of cities and pushing people and firms away from the cities.

REFERENCES

Arvis, J. F., M. A. Mustra, L. Ojala, B. Shepherd, and D. Saslavsky. 2012. *Connecting to Compete: Trade Logistics in the Global Economy*. Washington, DC: World Bank. http://www.worldbank .org/content/dam/Worldbank/document/Trade/LPI2014.pdf.

Defourny, P. 2017. *ESA Land Cover Climate Change Initiative: Land Cover Maps, v2.0.7*. Centre for Environmental Data, Rutherford Appleton Laboratory, Chilton, United Kingdom.

Fajgelbaum, P., and S. Redding. 2018. *Trade, Structural Transformation and Development: Evidence from Argentina 1869–1914*. http://www.econ.ucla.edu/pfajgelbaum/Argentina.pdf.

Herrera Dappe, M., and M. Lebrand. 2019. "The Spatial Effects of Logistics Interventions on the Economic Geography of Bangladesh." Policy Research Working Paper, World Bank, Washington, DC.

HPC (Hamburg Port Consulting), Sellhorn Engineering, and KS Consultants. 2015. *Strategic Master Plan for Chattogram Port*.

Hummels, D. L., and G. Schaur. 2013. "Time as a Trade Barrier." *American Economic Review* 103 (7): 2935-59.

Imbs, J., and I. Mejean. 2017. "Trade Elasticities." *Review of International Economics* 25 (2): 383-402.

Lall, S., and M. Lebrand. 2019. "Who Wins, Who Loses? Understanding the Spatially Differentiated Effects of Belt and Road within Central Asia." Policy Research Working Paper 8806, World Bank, Washington, DC.

7 Conclusions and Policy Direction

CONCLUSIONS

Rising wage demands and intensifying global competition are challenging the sustainability of Bangladesh's export-oriented growth model based on low wages. Logistics costs, which represent 4.5–47.9 percent of sales, make it difficult to compete in low-margin sectors like ready-made garments.

The weak state of logistics means that there is room to increase competitiveness through logistics-related interventions. Some inefficiencies are general and amenable to broad policy measures. Others are specific to particular sectors of the economy, regions, or locations; modes of transport; or components of logistics services.

The main horizontal issues are the congestion and unreliability of the logistics system. Congestion is evident across much of the country, especially in the Chattogram and Dhaka economic belt. Congestion and unreliability drive up logistics costs by increasing direct costs and pushing firms to hold large inventories. Congestion also imposes a high cost on society, accounting for more than half of the emissions of various pollutants. Congestion and unreliability partly reflect the failure of infrastructure investments to keep pace with growing demand as GDP surged. They also reflect the inefficient operation of key infrastructure, like Chattogram Port and railways, where the public sector plays an outsized role.

Bangladesh's logistics system is unsophisticated and inefficient. Efficient modern logistics systems are characterized by the use of different permutations of modes of transport in multimodal operations. Bangladesh's system is fragmented in terms of both transport modes and institutional responsibility. As a result, operators and service providers must deal with numerous licensing authorities, and shippers must use multiple service providers to ship goods. Fragmented service providers are characterized by low skills, poor quality of assets, and limited use of IT tools.

The market structure; weaknesses in the policy, regulatory, and business environments; and trade and transport procedures drive inefficiencies in logistics services in Bangladesh. The structure of the services markets is likely the most important reason for low quality and unreliable services. Operators of transport services mitigate the effects of competition by forming unions and associations and informally regulating market operations.

Another important reason for the sector's inefficiency is the lack of policies focusing on services. Policy and regulatory constraints and weaknesses in the business environment limit the role of the private sector in the operation and management of infrastructure and of foreign companies in service provision. Weakness in the enforcement of regulations and corruption, in the form of facilitation payments, also results in poor service levels.

Shippers demand an efficient and modern logistics system that caters to their business needs. The prevalence of facilitation payments to expedite the movement of goods suggests that there is demand for quicker processes and that shippers are willing to pay for them. The large share of in-house logistics service provision is also a sign that shippers demand sophisticated, high-quality services and are willing to pay for them.

Integrating Bangladesh's transport and logistics systems with the systems of neighboring countries, especially India, could yield huge benefits. Bangladesh could serve as a major junction for cross-border freight flows connecting Bhutan, India, Myanmar, and Nepal. Several regional initiatives are in place to integrate the transport and logistics systems of South Asian countries and integrate with southeast Asia, through Myanmar. These initiatives have not yet borne fruit, however, because of the misalignment of economic, technical, political economy, and regulatory regimes.

Investments and policy reforms to remove the inefficiencies in the logistics system would bring significant gains in exports growth. Different interventions distribute the gains across districts differently, but all of them leverage the comparative advantage and livability of Greater Dhaka, increasing its prominence in the country. The economic geography of Bangladesh and the transport network led to the northwest-southeast corridor being the backbone of the country, connecting all districts to Chattogram Port. Removing the logistics inefficiencies would increase the importance of the corridor, particularly of some sections. The freight demand model and the spatial general equilibrium model presented in this report can inform policy makers' decisions.

POLICY DIRECTION

The comprehensive diagnostic presented in this report yields one main conclusion: A system-wide approach is needed to increase logistics efficiency. This section provides high-level direction on the policy domains that may be considered when designing such an approach.

A well-rounded system-wide approach should be guided by a logistics strategy focused on infrastructure and services aimed at increasing logistics efficiency. The overarching objective of increasing logistics efficiency can be split into four interlinked objectives:

- developing a system-wide strategy aimed at increasing logistics efficiency
- improving the quality, capacity, and management of infrastructure.
- improving the quality and integration of logistics services.
- achieving seamless integration of regional logistics services.

Developing a system-wide strategy aimed at increasing logistics efficiency

Coordinating within the public sector and with the private sector

A successful strategy should ensure coordination among all public institutions involved in logistics and be co-developed with private sector shippers and service providers. International experience has shown that inclusive institutional arrangements can facilitate multidisciplinary decision making in logistics. Such arrangements include logistics councils and committees made up of senior representatives of a wide array of public sector entities, such as mode-specific ministries; ministries of planning, industry, trade, agriculture, economy, and finance; customs administrators; police and law enforcement; governance and anticorruption agencies. They are chaired by the country's highest executive authority, such as the president or prime minister.

Logistics councils and committees can be particularly effective at (a) coordinating interministerial priorities within budgetary, technical, legal, and other constraints; (b) monitoring the timely and cost-effective implementation of such priorities; (c) assessing systemwide performance improvements, by tracking selected key performance indicators; and (d) informing public policy through evidence-based research and consultations with concerned public and private parties. Countries that have implemented dedicated institutional arrangements of this kind include Australia the (Australian Logistics Council, the Transport and Logistics Centre, and the Integrated Logistics Network, and state-level freight logistics councils); Japan (the Japan Institute of Logistics Systems); Malaysia (the Malaysian Logistics Council); and Thailand (the National Logistics Committee).

Using evidence-based decision making

Policy makers need to think very carefully about where to invest, what to invest in, and what policies to implement. Investments in transport and logistics infrastructure have wider economic impacts. For example, they are not spatially neutral, as the concentration of people and economic activities gives rise to agglomeration benefits. Should future investments continue to favor the leading regions? Should policy try to relieve local operational constraints? How much investment should go to the preferred mode of transport compared with other modes? A transport and logistics master plan that identifies the mix of investments and policies that yield the greatest net benefits should be developed, considering all transport modes, both infrastructure and services, and the wider economic impacts of transport and logistics interventions. The master plan should be anchored in a transport model. The freight demand and spatial general equilibrium models developed for this study can be used in developing the integrated master plan.

The strategy should set measurable targets for progress to be continuously monitored. This study represents the first comprehensive effort to gather substantial data on freight flows, logistics costs, infrastructure, services, and institutions in Bangladesh. To continuously improve the logistics system, the public and private sectors need to collect and analyze data to monitor system performance. Policy makers need to build on the knowledge generated by this report by establishing a national system for data gathering, monitoring, and evaluation of system performance. They also need to nurture a culture of evidence-based decision making. Setting a logistics observatory—in association with one or more academic institutions, for example—linked to a logistics council or committee is one option for ensuring the sustainability of the effort.

Improving infrastructure quality, capacity, and management

Moving away from the build, neglect, rebuild mindset

The weak state of Bangladesh's transport infrastructure reduces the capacity of the network and the quality of logistics services. Lack of proper maintenance also leads to higher capital investment needs. Passage of the Road Maintenance Fund Board Act and inclusion of maintenance in sectoral policies are steps in the right direction, but they are not enough. The government needs to ensure adequate funding for maintenance and implementation of such policies.

Expanding the capacity of core transport and logistics infrastructure

Key components of the transport and logistics system are highly congested—and projected economic growth will further strain the system. Connectivity needs to be improved by expanding existing links and building new ones. The solution is not just to invest more, however, but to invest better, by focusing on the service gap instead of the infrastructure gap. Improving service requires much more than just capital expenditure. Improving the operation of the Chattogram and Mongla ports and Bangladesh Railways, for example, would expand their effective capacity. Investment decisions should be based on the integrated transport master plan.

Enhancing climate resilience

As a low-lying country, Bangladesh is particularly vulnerable to the effects of climate change. It lies in the path of monsoon storms and experiences extreme rains that often result in flooding. Scientific evidence on global warming suggests that both the frequency and the magnitude of extreme events will increase. Large sections of the transport network are already exposed to natural disasters. It is therefore important to build connectivity infrastructure that will be able to withstand such events, especially flooding. The Bangladesh transport system is overly dependent on a few nodes and links that intermediate flows between different parts of the country. Disruptions to traffic flows through the critical nodes and links would have devastating effects on the economy by disrupting important supply chains and slowing economic activity. Increasing resilience requires building climate-resilient infrastructure and adding redundancy to the system. Doing so may increase costs, but the costs of disruption to the economy and society could be much higher. The potential costs of disruption need to be included in project cost-benefit analyses.

Promoting multimodality through logistics clusters

Bangladesh has limited facilities for multimodal logistics. Measures to improve system performance should include identifying locations for multimodal terminals with storage and handling facilities and letting market forces determine prices. Clusters could be designed to complement and support the special economic zones agenda. Over time the terminals could be developed into logistics clusters or freight villages, which are common in economies with the best logistics performance. Cluster development would require close cooperation between the public and private sectors as well as with municipal authorities

Strengthening regulatory framework and enforcement

Some policies and regulations, well intended as they may be, inadvertently end up increasing traffic on roads. Examples include policies that limit the inland use of containers and policies that favor road transport over other modes. The government should ensure a level operating environment and the alignment of policies and regulations with the objective of improving logistics efficiency.

Lack of enforcement of axle-load regulations is damaging the roads. Overloading controls should be extended where available and established where they are not, through permanent weigh stations with weigh-in-motion capability, ideally operated under PPP arrangements. Whether on highways or at port locations, overloading fees assessed on offenders should reflect the cost of repairing the roads they damaged.

Rethinking and improving the paradigm for providing infrastructure services

The private sector plays a minimal role in the financing, management, and operation of infrastructure in Bangladesh. The government has been unsuccessful in attracting private participation in transport infrastructure in part because infrastructure is not included in the list of permitted foreign investments.

The government should prioritize the PPP framework to clarify the rules of engagement with the private sector when investing in infrastructure. The absence of such a framework reduces private sector confidence about executing projects through PPPs, scope for which exists across all parts of the logistics system.

Improving the quality and integration of logistics services

Increasing competition in logistics services markets

Competitive markets for logistics services would provide adequate incentives for service providers to improve the quality of their services, invest in technology and equipment, and provide integrated services. Associations, unions, and agents are distorting the functioning of the markets. The government should make the Bangladesh Competition Commission, established in 2016 to ensure competition, functional and independent.

Removing some of the constraints to the entry of foreign logistics firms would increase competition and raise the quality of service. Regulations that limit foreign firms from controlling the quality of the services they provide and the prices they can charge are setting high entry barriers that prevent the transfer of knowledge to local firms.

Upgrading regulations for logistics services

The regulatory regime for logistics services is outdated and patchy. Numerous agencies regulate different aspects of the system. Some agencies issue directives that make the overall regime unpredictable and nontransparent.

Basic principles should be adopted for regulating the sector, but regulation should be kept to a minimum and limited to issues relating to safety and market failures. Regulations should be easily accessible, simple, understandable, and consistent with transport and logistics policy goals. They should conform to bilateral, regional, and international agreements and offer clear guidelines and administrative structures for implementation and enforcement.

Strengthening enforcement of regulations

Poor enforcement of regulations can have severe consequences for the sustainability of infrastructure and services and the quality of services that the logistics system offers. Service providers exploit various loopholes to evade regulations, especially with regard to control of vehicle axle weights and vehicle and driver licensing. More investment is needed in the human resources, equipment, and facilities needed to enforce regulations.

Solutions to promote consistent implementation, interpretation, and enforcement of regulations can generally be implemented in the short term. Interventions to reduce the incidence of facilitation payments take longer, given the strong behavioral component of such initiatives and the obvious entrenched interests that would oppose reform.

The government should be as clear and transparent as possible when stating policies and issuing regulations related to logistics, in order to remove vagueness, ambiguity, and room for individual (especially idiosyncratic) discretion. There should be no or minimal room for different interpretations by different government officials.

Although it is not possible to eliminate corruption, the use of technology can help reduce it, by limiting opportunities for contact with officials. Options include electronic issuance and payment of traffic violations, use of machines for vehicle fitness inspection, and electronic issuance of driver licenses and slots on ferries. Technologies such as blockchain can help reduce or even eliminate opportunities to tamper with the certification process.

Increasing access to financing

A common challenge faced by operators is the lack of financing from the banking sector that would allow them to scale up their operations. Because their assets are mobile, the transport and logistics services sectors are considered risky. Policy measures are needed that allow operators who meet specific criteria (regarding vehicle standards, financial statements, operating procedures, and insurance, for example) to access bank financing. Creating a business environment in which banks would accept movable assets as collateral—which should include creating a tamper-proof property registry, as the government is aiming to do—would be a step in the right direction.

Across the world, countries have implemented schemes to modernize vehicles, vessels, and logistics services. Examples of fleet renewal policies include inducements offered in China, Germany Jordan, Pakistan, and Turkey to encourage operators to purchase newer and more efficient truck fleets (Lam, Sriram, and Khera 2019). The government of Bangladesh could consider similar policies.

Achieving seamless regional connectivity

Implementing integration agreements following best practices

Bangladesh could leverage its central location in South Asia to maximize the benefits from intermediate trade and freight flows with and between neighboring countries. It is already party to several regional connectivity initiatives, including the Bangladesh-China-India and Myanmar economic corridor; the Bangladesh, Bhutan, India and Nepal Motor Vehicle Agreement; the Protocol on Inland Water Transit and Trade (PIWTT); and a bilateral agreement with India. None of these agreements has been properly implemented, however. Their implementation requires that several measures be taken, including building infrastructure to at least the standards of the best performers in the region, harmonizing regulatory regimes, and integrating some systems, especially customs and border management.

Using international legal instruments for harmonization

Where regional agreements have not been negotiated to standardize or harmonize different aspects of transport and logistics infrastructure and services, Bangladesh could use international conventions and agreements as a starting point. It could prioritize several agreements, including some proposed by regional organizations, such as the South Asian Association for Regional Cooperation (SAARC) and the United Nations Economic and Social Commission for Asia and the Pacific (UNESCAP).

Recommended actions

Table 7.1 outlines the framework for improving and modernizing the logistics system.

TABLE 7.1 Recommended actions for improving and modernizing Bangladesh's logistics system

POLICY DOMAIN	POSSIBLE ACTIONS
Objective 1: Developing a system-wide strategy for increasing logistics efficiency	
Coordination within the public sector and with the private sector	• Develop inclusive institutional arrangements such as logistics councils or committees to develop and implement logistics strategy. • Involve private sector shippers and service providers in developing the strategy.
Evidence-based decision making	• Develop an integrated transport master plan that identifies the mix of investments and policies that yield the greatest net benefits. The master plan should consider all transport modes, infrastructure and services, infrastructure maintenance costs, and the wider economic impacts of transport and logistics interventions. • Develop a transport model for the master plan, and adopt it and maintain it to inform policy decisions. • Define key performance indicators for logistics. • Maintain a monitoring and evaluation system (for example, under a logistics observatory).
Objective 2: Improving the quality, capacity, and management of infrastructure	
Infrastructure maintenance	• Implement maintenance policies and actions included in the infrastructure master plans. • Allocate resources for infrastructure maintenance. Start by securing funds for the Road Maintenance Fund and making it operational. • Prioritize maintenance over new construction.
Infrastructure capacity	• Base decisions on capacity expansion on the integrated transport master plan. • Strengthen the capacity to implement projects. • Strengthen governance and increase competition in infrastructure construction. • Adopt modern practices to enhance climate resilience. • Develop alternative nodes and links across the transport system to increase redundancy and resilience based on robust analysis. • Develop logistics clusters at strategic locations with intermodal terminals.
Private sector participation	• Develop a robust and effective PPP framework. • Develop the domestic capital market and allow foreign financing of transport and logistics infrastructure. • Strengthen contract enforcement mechanisms. • Implement the landlord port model in Chattogram.
Design and enforcement of regulations	• Ensure that the tax system treats all transport modes equally or tilt the field in favor of cleaner modes (such as inland waterways). • Promote inland containerization by removing constraints to clearing goods outside sea ports and not treating containers as bonded goods. • Enforce limits on axle loads.
Objective 3: Improving the quality and integration of logistics services	
Market structure	• Make the Bangladesh Competition Commission functional and independent. • Enforce competition regulations in logistics service markets, letting market forces determine prices. • Make pricing regimes for different activities and services transparent.
Business environment	• Remove regulatory constraints that limit domestic and foreign private sector provision of logistics services. • Create the regulatory and business environment for logistics service providers to access bank financing. • Strengthen tax collection to create a level playing field for logistics service providers.
Design and enforcement of regulations	• Update and focus regulations on safety, the environment, and market failures in general. Refrain from interfering with market operation. • Issue regulations that are as clear and concrete as possible, to leave little room for discretion when interpreting them. • Make all regulations available online and easy to access for general public. • Implement technology solutions to improve the enforcement of regulations.
Objective 4: Achieving seamless regional connectivity	
Integration agreements	• Conduct conformity assessments to determine gaps in regional and international commitments. • Assess the economic impacts of regional and international agreements. • Use international legal instruments to harmonize regulatory regimes. • Integrate customs and border management systems with neighboring countries.
Infrastructure	• Build the infrastructure needed to interconnect with the transport networks of neighboring countries. • Build infrastructure to at least the standards of the best performers in the region.

Source: World Bank.

Freight Generation Survey

SAMPLING

The sampling frames used to design the sampling plan were the 2013 Economic Census Data and the 2008 Agriculture Census. The intent of the sampling plan was to collect sufficient data to estimate freight generation models for the sectors included in the model. The sample size was set at 4,000 observations. To ensure that it represented the wide range of conditions, the sample was stratified by sector, geographical area, and establishment size (measured by employment).

The emphasis of the data collection exercise was on freight-intensive sectors. Ten such sectors were identified, based on the two-digit level Bangladesh Standard Industrial Classification (agriculture; wholesale; retail; transport and storage; manufacturing; accommodation and food; mining and quarrying; construction; electricity, gas, steam, and air conditioning supply; and water supply, sewerage, and waste management). The freight activity for 4 of these 10 sectors (mining and quarrying; construction; electricity, gas, steam and air conditioning supply; and water supply, sewerage, and waste management) is either region specific (mining, electricity and gas), or changeable over time (construction, water supply and sanitation). Given the negligible share of these sectors in terms of establishments and employment (less than 1 percent), they were excluded from the study.

The 4,000 samples were allocated across the six freight-intensive sectors based on the heterogeneity of the sectors. For instance, the freight pattern of the retail sector is more homogeneous than the pattern for manufacturing. Retailers typically receive their products from their distributors and suppliers and sell them to consumers. In contrast, metal and food manufacturers have very different freight patterns. They have very different suppliers, clientele, and production technologies. It therefore made sense to allocate more samples to manufacturing and fewer to retail than under proportional sampling. By the same logic, more samples were allocated to the wholesale, transport and storage, and food sectors, and fewer samples were allocated to the agriculture sector than under proportional sampling.

Geographic coverage was based on two criteria: inclusion of districts that are major contributors to freight but lack of bias toward major freight-generating districts. Twenty-six districts were selected for data collection (Barishal, Brahamanbaria, Bogura, Chandpur, Chattogram, Cumilla, Dhaka,

Gazipur, Gopalganj, Jeshore, Khulna, Lakshmipur, Narsingdi, Moulvibazar, Mymensingh, Narail, Narayanganj, Noakhali, Pabna, Rajshahi, Rangpur, Satkhira, Shariatpur, Sirajganj, Sylhet, and Tangail). Once the districts were selected, the number of observations per district was allocated based on the sectoral composition.

Establishment size is considered a proxy for the level of technology. Larger establishments tend to adopt more sophisticated technology than smaller establishments. A significant number of economic establishments in Bangladesh are microenterprises, with just one or two employees. Given the very small scale of these establishments, they are likely to produce goods that are sold locally. As the intent of this study was to develop models that depict inter-district freight flow, it did not consider microenterprises. To ensure sufficient establishment size coverage, the sample was stratified across seven employment ranges (2–5, 6–10, 11–25, 26–50, 51–150, 151–500, and more than 500).

SURVEY INSTRUMENT

The freight-generation analysis was based on information collected from the following survey.

Freight Generation and Freight Trip Generation Study for Establishments

Information you provide here will be kept confidential and will be used for planning purposes only

Disclaimer: This survey is organized by the World Bank to benefit the Bangladesh economy by improving the freight performance

1. Survey ID

Interviewer ID: _____

Survey ID: _____

2. PERSON CONDUCTING THE INTERVIEW

Name: _____   Position: _____

Phone number: _____   E-mail: _____

3. ESTABLISHMENT INFORMATION

Name of the market: _____   Sampling rate (%): _____

Name of the establishment: _____   BSIC code (4-digit): _____

Complete Address: _____

City: _____   Division: _____   District/Zila: _____

Sub-District/Thana: _____   Union: _____   Mauza: _____

4. PERSON BEING INTERVIEWED

Name: _____   Position: _____

Phone number: _____   Cell phone number: _____   E-mail: _____

5. MAIN BUSINESS ACTIVITY TYPE (Use Manual 1 for Business Activity Type*)

Main business activity type*: _____   Specify (if not in Manual 1): _____

Complete description of the business: _____

6. TYPE OF ESTABLISHMENT (Check ✓ appropriate box)

| Single Establishment ☐ | Headquarters ☐ | Branch ☐ |

7. NUMBER OF PEOPLE CURRENTLY EMPLOYED AT THIS ADDRESS

	Full time	Part time	Casual	Owner	Unpaid member
Total number of employees in a typical day	_____	_____	_____	_____	_____

Is the work done at the premises performed in shifts?   YES ☐   Number of shifts per day: _____   NO ☐

If checked YES, total number of employees per shift: Shift 1 _____   Shift 2 _____   Shift 3 _____   Shift 4 _____

8. AREA OF THE ESTABLISHMENT

Area of the land occupied by the establishment	Total gross land area/gross floor area	Units (Sq.ft, Acres, Decimal)
	_____	

9. DOES YOUR ESTABLISHMENT CURRENTLY OWN/LEASE ANY VEHICLES   YES ☐   NO ☐

If checked YES go to Section-10, Else go to Section-11

10. NUMBER OF VEHICLES <u>OWNED/LEASED</u> (Use Manual 2 for Vehicle Type*)

If no information is available use "NA" for Not Available. If the answer is zero, use "0".

Vehicle type*	Number of vehicles owned	Number of vehicles leased	Number of axles	Number of tyres	other comments

11. FREIGHT TRIP GENERATION (Use Manual 2 for Vehicle Type*)

AVERAGE NUMBER OF VEHICLE TRIPS MADE TO/FROM THIS ADDRESS BY VEHICLE TYPE

If no information is available use "NA" for Not Available. If the answer is zero, use "0".

Vehicle type*	Average number of vehicles **COMING IN** to this address	Average number of vehicles **GOING OUT** from this address	Time Unit (Check ✓ appropriate box)
			per day ☐ per week ☐ per month ☐
			per day ☐ per week ☐ per month ☐
			per day ☐ per week ☐ per month ☐
			per day ☐ per week ☐ per month ☐
			per day ☐ per week ☐ per month ☐

12. FREIGHT GENERATION (Use Manual 1 for Business Activity*)

TOP FIVE TYPES OF CARGO <u>COMING IN</u> AND <u>GOING OUT</u> TO/FROM THIS ADDRESS   per day ☐   per week ☐   per month ☐

Type of cargo **COMING IN**	Total shipment size for time period	Average shipment size per delivery	Unit (tons/boxes/ pallets/m³)	Total number of deliveries for time period	Business activity at major origin*	Travel time by cargo (T, unit: **hours**)				Point of entry for import (e.g., port name)
						% of cargo travel T <= 1 hr. in BD	% of cargo travel 1 < T <= 3 hr. in BD	% of cargo travel T > 3 hr. in BD	% of cargo **imported**	
1.										
2.										
3.										
4.										
5.										

Type of cargo **GOING OUT**	Total shipment size for time period	Average shipment size per delivery	Unit (tons/boxes/ pallets/m³)	Total number of deliveries for time period	Business activity at major destination*	Travel time by cargo (T, unit: hours)				Point of exit for export (e.g., port name)
						% of cargo travel T <= 1 hr. in BD	% of cargo travel 1 < T <= 3 hr. in BD	% of cargo travel T > 3 hr. in BD	% of cargo **exported**	
1.										
2.										
3.										
4.										
5.										

13. MODE SHARE BY SHIPMENT SIZE (WEIGHT/VOLUME/PALLETS/BOXES)

Main mode of transportation	Mode share of deliveries from/to other districts					Other comments
	Road	Rail	Waterway	Air	Others (bicycle)	
Cargo **COMING IN**						
Cargo **GOING OUT**						

14. DO YOU OBSERVE ANY SEASONAL VARIATIONS   YES ☐   NO ☐

If checked YES go to Section-15, Else go to Section-16.

15. SEASONAL CHANGES

	Mode of transportation (Check ✔ appropriate box)				
	Road	Rail	Waterways	Air	Others (bicycle)
For cargo **COMING IN**, what are the top two primary modes used during Summer (May – October)?					
For cargo **COMING IN**, what are the top two primary modes used during Winter (November – April)?					
For cargo **GOING OUT**, what are the top two primary modes used during Summer (May – October)?					
For cargo **GOING OUT**, what are the top two primary modes used during Winter (November – April)?					

16. GENERAL COMMENTS

We Appreciate Your Time

APPENDIX B

Econometric Models of Freight Generation

The explanatory variable in the models is full-time equivalent (FTE) employees. Full-time includes both full-time employees and owners; non-full-time employees include all types of part-time employees, including casual and unpaid employees. The number of FTE employees is calculated assuming a non-full-time employee contribution to freight generation of 45 percent of the full-time employee contribution:

$$\text{FTE} = \text{full-time employment} + 0.45 * \text{non-full-time employment}. \quad \text{(B.1)}$$

Four types of models were estimated.

Linear models assume a proportional relationship between freight generation in establishment i in sector m (y_{in}) and FTE employment (x_{im}) in the establishment. Some models also include a constant parameter that adds a constant rate of trips produced independently of the effect of the explanatory variables considered. The linear model takes the following form:

$$y_{in} = \beta x_{in}. \quad \text{(B.2)}$$

Linear-logarithmic models assume that an establishment's freight generation is proportional to the natural logarithm of the establishment's FTE employment. The linear-logarithmic model takes the following form:

$$y_{in} = \alpha + \beta \ln x_{in}. \quad \text{(B.3)}$$

Exponential models assume that the marginal effect of FTE employment produces an exponential increase in the amount of freight generated by an establishment. The exponential model takes the following form:

$$y_{in} = e^{\left(\alpha + \frac{S^2}{2} + \beta x_{in}\right)} \quad \text{(B.4)}$$

where s^2 represents the mean squared error of the estimation.

The *logarithmic-logarithmic model*, also called a *power function*, assumes that the amount of freight an establishment generates increases to the power of the FTE employment. The logarithmic-logarithmic model takes the following form:

$$y_{in} = e^{\left(\alpha + \frac{S^2}{2}\right)} x_{in}^{\beta}. \quad \text{(B.5)}$$

APPENDIX C

Econometric Results of Freight Generation Models

TABLE C.1 **Results of linear model for freight generation**

BSIC	DESCRIPTION	FREIGHT ATTRACTION (KILOGRAMS/DAY)			FREIGHT PRODUCTION (KILOGRAMS/DAY)		
		β	T-STAT	OBSERVATIONS	β	T-STAT	OBSERVATIONS
Agriculture							
01	Crop and animal production and related	6.04	6.72	324	7.20	14.78	320
03	Fishing and aquaculture	5.05	3.29	79	18.03	2.62	76
Manufacturing							
13	Textiles	n.a	n.a	n.a	39.59	6.44	90
15	Manufacture of leather and related products	17.53	11.51	15	n.a	n.a	n.a
22	Rubber and plastics products	131.99	4.06	36	393.09	4.59	35
24	Basic metals	127.96	2.91	28	32.92	2.27	13
32	Other manufacturing	21.55	3.39	12	n.a	n.a	n.a
Wholesale							
46	Trade (no motor vehicles or motorcycles)	66.37	2.64	585	n.a	n.a	n.a
Retail							
45	Repair of motor vehicles and motorcycles	n.a	n.a	n.a	12.33	3.05	28
Transport							
52	Warehousing and support activities	n.a	n.a	n.a	1,022.83	5.80	81
Food							
56	Food and beverage service	52.16	42.82	489	48.95	13.36	457

Source: World Bank analysis.
Note: n.a. = not applicable.

TABLE C.2 **Results of best nonlinear models for freight generation**

BSIC	DESCRIPTION	FREIGHT ATTRACTION (KILOGRAMS/DAY)					FREIGHT PRODUCTION (KILOGRAMS/DAY)				
		α	T-STAT	β	T-STAT	OBSERVATIONS	α	T-STAT	β	T-STAT	OBSERVATIONS
Manufacturing											
10–12	Food, beverages, and tobacco	2.70	5.48	1.05	7.99	210	3.06	7.14	1.02	8.69	186
13	Textiles	1.42	2.32	1.19	9.74	85	n.a	n.a	n.a	n.a	n.a
14	Wearing apparel (ready-made garments)	n.a	n.a	1.32	21.15	131	n.a	n.a	1.18	30.05	128
15	Manufacture of leather and related products	n.a	n.a	n.a	n.a	n.a	n.a	n.a	1.63	23.58	17
16–18	Wood and related products	3.16	3.39	1.22	4.44	42	2.03	2.15	1.46	5.29	38
23	Other nonmetallic mineral products	4.46	4.01	1.43	6.09	89	5.25	6.42	1.24	7.32	80
25	Fabricated metal products (no machinery)	2.35	2.72	1.30	4.70	51	n.a	n.a	2.03	10.99	25
26–30	Machinery and equipment[a]	n.a	n.a	1.72	13.25	19	n.a	n.a	2574	2.34	14
31	Furniture	4.62	17.77	1.02	11.35	240	3.14	7.65	0.91	6.72	293
32	Other manufacturing	n.a	n.a	n.a	n.a	n.a	3.14	7.80	0.92	6.95	300
Wholesale											
46	Trade (no motor vehicles or motorcycles)	n.a	n.a	n.a	n.a	n.a	5.45	22.12	0.89	8.57	465
Retail											
45	Repair of motor vehicles and motorcycles	n.a	n.a	1.69	8.37	29	n.a	n.a	n.a	n.a	n.a
47	Retail trade (no motor vehicles or motorcycles)	1.81	7.15	1.13	10.14	721	2.18	9.72	0.95	9.55	718
Transport											
49	Land transport and via pipelines	n.a	n.a	3.29	9.04	15	n.a	n.a	2.88	8.81	10
52	Warehousing and support activities	n.a	n.a	2.36	14.67	79	n.a	n.a	n.a	n.a	n.a
53	Postal and courier activities	1.59	3.36	1.30	7.03	229	1.88	4.30	1.18	6.95	228

Source: World Bank analysis.
Note: n.a. = not applicable.
a. Linear-logarithmic model. All other models are power model.

APPENDIX D

Estimation of Origin-Destination

FREIGHT ORIGIN DESTINATION SYNTHESIS

The freight origin destination synthesis (FODS) assumes that the total flow of cargo from district i to district j for commodity $k \left(m_{ij}^k \right)$ follows a doubly constrained gravity model:[1]

$$m_{ij}^k = O_i^k D_j^k A_i^k B_j^k f_{ij} \tag{D.1}$$

where O_i^k and D_j^k are freight production and attraction for commodity k at districts i and j, respectively; A_i^k and B_j^k are balancing factors; and $f_{ij} = e^{-\beta^k c_{ij}}$ is a negative exponential deterrence function of cost c_{ij} with β^k as the impedance or gravity parameter for commodity k. The cost is independent of the commodity.

The model seeks to estimate the parameters of the demand model so that the resulting traffic flows resemble the observed traffic in the network. To do so, it assigns total truck trips to the network to obtain a set of estimated truck traffic volumes, which are compared with the observed truck traffic using observed traffic volume. The total number of truck trips from district i to district j is calculated as follows:

$$\sum_k z_{ij}^k = \sum_k x_{ij}^k + y_{ij} \tag{D.2}$$

where x_{ij}^k is the total number of loaded trips carrying commodity k from i to j, computed as the ratio between the total flow of the cargo of commodity k from i to j and the average payload from i to j, $\dfrac{m_{ij}^k}{a^{ij}}$, and y_{ij} is the total number of empty trips from i to j.

Number of loaded trips is directly determined by the commodity flow from i to j. Empty trips are typically generated in the opposite direction. To account for these trips, the FODS uses the model originally formulated by Noortman and Van Es (1978), which considers the probability of empty trips returning from j to i (p). The total number of truck trips from i to j is recalculated as follows:

$$\sum_k z_{ij}^k = \sum_k \left(x_{ij}^k + p x_{ji}^k \right), \tag{D.3}$$

which can be written as follows:

$$\sum_k z_{ij}^k = \sum_k \left(\frac{m_{ij}^k}{a^{ij}} + p\frac{m_{ji}^k}{a^{ji}} \right). \tag{D.4}$$

For the assignment needed in the origin-destination synthesis, the FODS uses a proportional route choice: The flow is a function of the proportion of traffic flow traveling from i to j using link l. These proportionality factors $\left(\bar{P}_{ij}^l \right)$ are computed using an all-or-nothing assignment that assumes that the traffic takes the shortest path. The estimated traffic flow in link l becomes

$$V_l^e = \sum_{i,j,k} z_{ij}^k \bar{P}_{ij}^l = \sum_{i,j,k} \left(\frac{m_{ij}^k}{a^{ij}} + p\frac{m_{ji}^k}{a^{ji}} \bar{P}_{ij}^l \right). \tag{D.5}$$

Based on the observed counts, the optimization process is initialized with starting values for parameters β and p and then recomputed to improve the agreement between estimated, V_l^e and observed truck traffic V_l^o. The intent is to minimize the effort function (F_v) (that is, the sum of the squared differences between the observed and estimated flows):

$$F_v = \sum_l \left(V_l^o - V_l^e \right)^2. \tag{D.6}$$

The procedure stops when the parameters β and p converge and there is no more improvement in the function F_v.

An important feature of the freight demand model at the core of the FODS is the relation between the parameter p and the percent of empty trips in the area, P_e. As Holguín-Veras and Thorson (2003) show, p and P_e are related by equations (D.7) and (D.8):

$$P_e = \frac{p}{1-p} \tag{D.7}$$

and

$$p = \frac{P_e}{1+P_e}. \tag{D.8}$$

The payload (a_{ij}), the empty trip parameter (p), and the proportionality factors $\left(\bar{P}_{ij}^l \right)$ are independent of the commodity. Hence p gives an average empty trip parameter for all commodities together.

Figure D.1 shows the parameter estimation process for multicommodity FODS. The first step in is to sort the commodities in descending order of freight generation (the sum of O_i^k and D_j^k for all districts), so that the first iteration for commodity k loads the network with the predominant commodity. For the second commodity, the estimated flows from the first and second commodity are added to the network. In the third iteration of commodity k, the estimated flows sum all top three commodity flows and so on until all K commodities are added to the estimated flows.

The next step is to estimate the empty trip model parameter (p) by minimizing F_v with respect to p for a given vector β. This iteration process is repeated until the convergence for all β^k and p are met.

FIGURE D.1

Estimation procedure for multicommodity freight origin-destination synthesis (FODS)

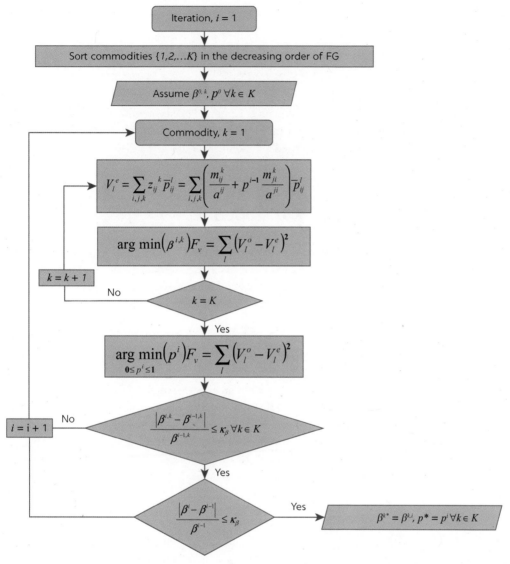

Source: World Bank analysis.

TRAVEL TIME ESTIMATION

A critical input for the FODS are the link transport costs, which are used to estimate the travel impedance between districts along the shortest paths (c_{ij}) and assign the estimated origin-destination matrix to the network based on all-or-nothing assignment. In the absence of transport cost data along each link, link costs can be estimated using distances or travel times. Travel times provide a better metric for link costs than distances, because they capture the level of service and congestion on the links.

The link costs adopted are the travel times in hours estimated from GPS data. Probe vehicles instrumented with GPS devices traveled along roads at peak-hour and free-flow conditions to gather speed data. The GPS data collected were processed to estimate the average speed of vehicles traveling on a given 1-kilometer segment of road. Speeds were estimated by using the average travel time and length for the road segment, as shown in equation D.9, where n refers to the number of observations in a road segment:

$$\text{Space} - \text{mean speed} = \frac{\text{distance traveled}}{\text{average travel time}} = \frac{d}{\sum_i t_i \big/ n}. \tag{D.9}$$

The estimated speeds for prevailing conditions (including congestion effects) range from 11.9 to 67.9 kilometers an hour. Speeds on all links in a district were assumed to have the same uniform distribution. Links that were not covered by the GPS data were assigned a random speed from the distribution of speeds in the district.

PORT OF ENTRY/EXIT MODELS

The FODS focuses on the domestic transport of freight. Hence freight flows associated with imports and exports must be removed from the traffic counts using port of entry/exit models, which estimate the freight traffic between international ports of entry/exit (land ports, airports, and seaports) and districts in Bangladesh.

One port of entry/exit model is constructed for each district with border posts or custom houses. Each port of entry/exit has two models: an import model, which is assumed to be an origin-constrained gravity model that estimates the destination of the import flow, and an export model, which is assumed to be a destination-constrained gravity model that estimates the flows from the origin districts to the port of exit.

The corresponding flows between districts and ports of entry/exit are assumed to be proportional to employment at firms with more than 25 employees in the manufacturing, wholesale, and transport sectors.

Port of entry model

Equation D.10 shows the flow of cargo imported through port of entry q (I_q) that is transported to other districts in Bangladesh:

$$m_{qi} = I_q \frac{E_i \exp\left(\beta c_{qi}\right)}{\sum_j E_j \exp\left(\beta c_{qj}\right)}. \tag{D.10}$$

where E_i is employment in manufacturing, wholesale, and transport in firms with more than 25 employees at district i and m_{qi} and c_{qi} represent cargo (weight) movement and cost from port q to district i, respectively.

Port of exit model

Equation D.11 shows the flow of cargo exported through port of entry q (Ex_q) that is transported from other districts in Bangladesh to q:

$$m_{iq} = Ex_q \frac{E_i \exp\left(\beta c_{iq}\right)}{\sum_j E_j \exp\left(\beta c_{jq}\right)} \tag{D.11}$$

Equation D.12 shows the truck flows between the port of entry q and district j:

$$z_{qj} = \frac{m_{qj}}{a^{qj}} + p\frac{m_{jq}}{a^{jq}} .$$

(D.12)

Using the β and p obtained from a single-commodity FODS, the trips between the port of entry and all districts are assigned to the network using all-or-nothing assignment. The port of entry/exit truck flows are removed from the traffic counts used to run the FODS. They are also removed from the freight generation before the FODS is run to estimate the origin-destination matrix.

NOTE

1. In the single commodity FODS, the superscript k disappears.

REFERENCES

Holguín-Veras, J., and E. Thorson. 2003. "Practical Implications of Modeling Commercial Vehicle Empty Trips." *Transportation Research Record: Journal of the Transportation Research Board* 1833: 87–94.

Noortman, H.J., and J. Van Es. 1978. *Traffic Model.* Manuscript for the Dutch Freight Transport Model.

Estimation of Private Logistics Costs

Based on the understanding gained from the surveys and in-depth interviews of firms, the study team estimated the logistics costs for different functions across the value chain. These costs were derived for the production and sale of 1 ton of finished goods. Conversion ratios were calculated for the quantity (in tons) of raw material required to manufacture 1 ton of finished goods. The logistics costs for each function are expressed as percentages of sales realized from the sale of 1 ton of finished goods.

Transport costs were estimated as follows:

- Step 1: Based on the 2012 Survey of Manufacturing Industries, the population census, and interactions with industry players, the study team mapped the key regions manufacturing finished goods, raw material sourcing regions, and consumption centers.
- Step 2: Based on the location of raw material sourcing regions, manufacturing plants and consumption centers, the study team mapped typical routes and corresponding lead distances.
- Step 3: Based on the average trucking tariffs prevalent in the market for different routes, the study team calculated the cost to transport the required inputs to the factory and the finished goods to buyers.

Warehousing costs were estimated as follows:

- Step 1: The warehousing space requirements for storage of raw materials were derived based on the number of inventory days and the typical area required to store 1 ton of raw material. The warehousing space requirement for finished goods was calculated using a similar procedure for raw materials.
- Step 2: Based on warehousing rental and management cost (the cost per ton per square foot) collected through the surveys, the study team calculated the cost to store 1 ton of finished goods and the raw material required to produce it.

Handling costs for loading/unloading of raw materials and finished goods were calculated based on the unit rate (Tk per ton), as informed by user industries.

Trade facilitation costs were estimated as follows:

- Step 1: The port tariffs, freight forwarding rates, customs handling rates, and other handling and storage costs incurred at port and off-docks during the import/export of goods were considered to calculate trade facilitation–related costs. The unit costs for import/export-related charges were sourced from primary interactions with Chattogram Port and off-docks in Chattogram and from the landside tariff sheet obtained from Mitsui O.S.K. Lines.
- Step 2: These charges were converted from Tk per container to Tk per ton based on the quantity of product carried.
- Step 3: For raw materials, the conversion ratio was used to calculate the total import expenses incurred in producing 1 ton of finished product.

Inventory carrying costs were calculated based on the lead distances used to calculate transport costs, the inventory days used to calculate warehousing costs, the average waiting time at port for clearance, and the cost of capital in Bangladesh (the prevalent interest rate for working capital of 18 percent was used).

Corridors and Regions Covered by GPS Data on Truck Movements

MAP F.1

Corridors and regions of Bangladesh covered by GPS data on truck movements

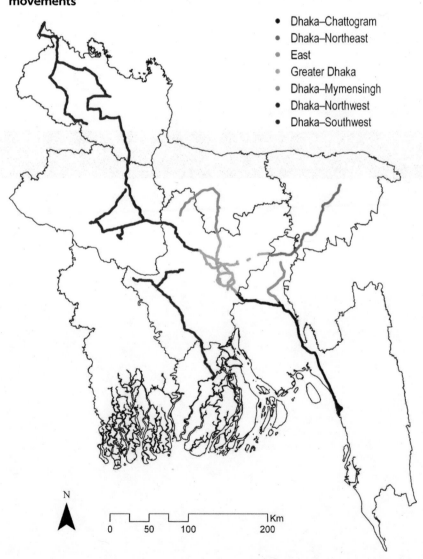

- Dhaka–Chattogram
- Dhaka–Northeast
- East
- Greater Dhaka
- Dhaka–Mymensingh
- Dhaka–Northwest
- Dhaka–Southwest

N

0   50   100   200   Km

Source: World Bank analysis.